6/3/07

*w/ love ... to
Thoughts
Old friend love Nancy
Phillip & Lily*

WORKING
FOR YOURSELF

WORKING

FOR YOURSELF

A Guide to Success for People Who Work Outside the 9 to 5 World

Phillip Namanworth
and Gene Busnar

Illustrated by Barbara Samuels

McGraw-Hill Book Company

New York   St. Louis   San Francisco   Bogotá   Guatemala   Hamburg   Lisbon
Madrid   Mexico   Montreal   Panama   Paris   San Juan   São Paulo   Tokyo   Toronto

2 3 4 5 6 7 8 9 DOCDOC 8 7 6

ISBN 0-07-009346-6 {PBK}
ISBN 0-07-009347-4 {HC}

LIBRARY OF CONGRESS CATALOGING IN PUBLICATION DATA

Namanworth, Phillip.
Working for yourself.
Bibliography: p.
Includes index.
1. Self-employed.   I. Busnar, Gene.   II. Title.
HD8036.N35 1985   658'.041   84-11314
ISBN 0-07-009346-6 (Pbk)
ISBN 0-07-009347-4 (HC)

BOOK DESIGN BY PATRICE FODERO

For Nancy and Elizabeth

Table of Contents

Table of Contents

Table of Contents

Acknowledgments

We want to thank all the people we interviewed for sharing their stories and insights with us. We'd particularly like to thank the following for their expertise: Don Reilly, David Feinstein, Lura Brookins, Erna Ferris, Carol O'Rourke, Bernard Meltzer, Bill Bresnan, Al Ries, Newton Frank, Adele Scheele, Marge Baxter, Martha Friedman, Maggie Cadman, Angelo Valenti, and Seymour Feig.

For lending a helping hand, thanks also go to: Kathryn Lance, Ralph Bogertman, Adele Kaplan, Erna Helwig, Brad Ross, Alan Rosenbloom, Barbara Samuels, Ivan Berger, Daniel Gildesgame, Nick Ramoundos for designing the charts on pages 14, 15, and 23, and Jamie Forbes for editing the proposal.

Special thanks to Merrilee Heifetz, our agent, and to our fine and patient editors at McGraw-Hill, PJ Haduch and Ken Stuart.

A special word of gratitude to Rita Namanworth, and Irving & Nadya Busnar.

Introduction

"How do you do it?" our nine-to-five friends often ask. "How do you make yourself work every day? How do you find enough paying assignments to make a good living? How do you keep from going stir crazy working alone?" Truthfully, we've learned many of our own lessons by trial and error. How much easier it all would be, we thought, if people who work for themselves had some kind of guidelines on which to build their careers. Even if preexisting rules don't apply, every thriving freelancer we know uses a set of self-imposed parameters as a frame of reference. We decided to develop a flexible framework within which those who work for themselves could find a space for their own uniqueness.

We started out with our own personal experiences and those of our friends. We then developed a wide-ranging set of questions that we asked self-employed people from every walk of life. We asked them how they structured their time, how they handled their money, how they found new clients and every other relevant question we could think of. We also interviewed experts of all kinds who were familiar with the problems of the self-employed. We spoke to time-efficiency specialists, business managers, financial consultants, career counselors, and psychologists (interestingly, many of these experts work for themselves). We also spoke to reps and others who find work for freelancers, as well as business people who frequently hire freelancers. In the course of our research we read countless books and articles on the many subjects which have an impact on a freelancer's career and lifestyle—everything from business management to Zen. We spent hundreds of hours sifting out all this accumulated knowledge and wisdom and applying it in our consultations and seminars. In the process, we discovered that there is as much to be learned from the humor and poignancy of people's experiences as from nuts-and-bolts information. As we constantly tell each other, we never would have gotten into all this if we couldn't take a joke.

During the course of our research we found that people refer to themselves as either freelancers, consultants, self-employed, or owners of their own businesses. **For the purposes of this book, we use the terms _freelance_ and _self-employed_ to mean anyone who works for himself or herself.**

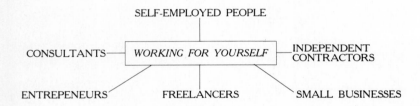

Until recently, the term "freelance" was applied most often to those in the arts. But as we spoke to self-employed women and men in different fields, we found that the problems of working independently are pretty much the same. You have to create your own structure, pay for your own medical insurance, and deal with the insecurities of not having a regular paycheck. The point is this: If you work for yourself—either full or part time—or are considering it as an option somewhere down the road, this book is for you.

Whether you're a graphic artist just out of school; a musician who'd like to get more recognition; a computer programmer who has worked nine-to-five for ten years and is now becoming a consultant; a freelance writer who has been paying the rent for ten years and wants a more financially rewarding career; a mother with school-age children who wants to turn her knack for exotic cooking into a part-time catering service; a craftsman who is considering early retirement to start his own custom furniture business; or a schoolteacher who has finally gotten up the nerve to get some of her short stories published, you will find invaluable information presented with compassion by two people who understand what you're up against.

The principles and techniques in this book are designed to help you make more money, have more time for yourself, and achieve your career and lifestyle objectives. We have put together the first comprehensive program that deals with the situations (problematic and otherwise) that self-employed people come up against. We suggest that you read the book in its entirety and complete all the exercises and questionnaires for best results. There is a lot of material on these pages and you'll have to digest it at your own pace. Some readers may choose to skip around or seek out specific information as the need arises. Obviously, this approach is better than nothing, yet it doesn't really address what we feel to be the key issues. It's not so much specific information that people lack, as overall solutions to pervasive problems.

In writing this book, we kept asking ourselves and each other how to effectively bridge the gap between knowing and doing. It would have been relatively simple to just tell people what to do, but that would have been missing the real point. We decided it is far more helpful to get people to ask the right questions and develop the motivation to find solutions that work for them. After all, successful self-employment is about discovering your uniqueness and taking it out into the world. If it's exact rules you're after, maybe you'd be better off working nine-to-five. But if you're looking for more control over your own destiny, you've come to the right place.

1

What It Takes to Be Successfully Self-Employed

Did you ever have a job in which you could get up for work whenever you wanted, set your own hours or take a day off in the middle of the week to catch a movie? If you've spent some time working for yourself, then you've enjoyed these and many other amenities. Just think of some of the typical nine-to-five hassles you avoid: those horrendous rush-hour traffic jams; those back-biting, ulcer-producing office politics; and those twelve o'clock lunch breaks that come two hours before you really feel like eating. Whenever your nine-to-five friends tell you how fortunate you are to work for yourself, you know exactly what kinds of advantages they have in mind. Still, as much as we value our freedom, we have been known to fret about the relative lack of security and order in our lives.

"God, you're so lucky," a freelance photographer said to her friend who works nine-to-five. "You know what time you'll be getting up tomorrow morning for work, while I'm going to have to wrestle myself out of bed and force myself to be productive. If you take a long lunch, you've gotten the best of your boss. But if

I do the same, I'm really only cheating myself." The photographer then went on to complain about a $700 doctor's bill that was overdue. An expense, she was quick to add, that her friend would never have to worry about because of the medical insurance provided by her employer.

Let's face it. Working for yourself isn't always as footloose and fancy-free as it is sometimes characterized. In order to establish and maintain successful careers, self-employed people must be able to function effectively in a number of complex areas they are frequently unequipped to handle. We have come across highly talented men and women who never even approach their potentials because they have no idea how to market their best skills or to present themselves properly at meetings with clients. We have seen far too many beginning freelancers abandon promising careers because they never learned to deal with the anxieties of working on a project-to-project basis. Even experienced freelancers sometimes find it necessary to take nine-to-five jobs just to impose some external structure on their lives and to feel the inner glow that a regular paycheck can provide. But many of them leave these temporary havens of security only to return to freelancing. For in spite of all its difficulties, the freelance life allows people the freedom to design a world of work that reflects their own unique personalities, talents, and aspirations.

If you are interested in becoming successful, you need to create and perpetuate a lifestyle that is truly an expression of who you are and what you want to achieve. You have already probably spent years developing the tools of your trade. Are you willing to take a few hours to learn the tools of successful self-employment? If so, we can give you the skills you need to reach your potential.

Since we are great believers in defining goals, we want you to be clear on what our primary goal in this book is: *to help you become successful*. We want to join you in creating a program that is custom designed to suit you and your particular career. Together, we will take stock of how you are operating in those vital areas that have the greatest impact on your work. You will learn to make the most of your strengths as your discover new and relatively simple ways to improve your functioning in any problem areas. You will develop simple and effective ways to handle the business side of your freelance career, even if you've always shied away from finances and things of that nature. You will find out how successful freelancers overcome frustration and anxiety. You will learn how to negotiate the best terms with clients who are frequently in no hurry to pay you.

Our comprehensive program includes specific advice and tips that pertain to virtually any situation you might come across. But the greatest benefit will come to those readers who use this information with an understanding of the three underlying principles that form the foundation for successful self-employment:

1.   You are your own business.

2.   You can overcome obstacles by effective planning.

3.   You determine your own success.

Be your own business

Principle 1:
YOU ARE YOUR OWN BUSINESS

WE ARE ALWAYS AMAZED WHEN FREELANCERS TELL us that it took them five or ten years to realize that they ought to start treating their work in a businesslike manner. If our aim is to earn a living by marketing our services and products, how else can we view ourselves *except as* independent business people? Nevertheless, far too many freelancers have stifled themselves in the past by treating the business side of their careers with indifference and even contempt. This attitude prevents them from reaching their objectives. It can also generate a negative response from potentially lucrative clients.

The "I Am an Artiste" Attitude

As the president of Freelance File, Inc., Don Reilly is actively involved with the placement of freelance artists and graphic designers. Like many other professionals who deal with freelancers on a day-to-day basis, Reilly finds that they often make "lousy salesmen, lousy businessmen, and lousy accountants. Some freelancers in the arts seem to believe that business is the closest thing to sin," Reilly observes. "They take the following attitude: I am an artiste and I just don't want to be bothered with the mundane pursuits of business."

If you are not particularly interested in making your living from your art, you can follow the example of composer Charles

Ives who sold insurance by day so that he could pursue his musical career on a purely aesthetic basis. However, if one of your objectives is to sell your work for profit, you require a business policy to achieve that objective—no matter how artistic or high-minded your work might be.

If you want your career to be self-fulfilling and profitable, you need to get comfortable with the notion that you will have to do whatever it takes to achieve these goals. This does not mean that you are going to have to compromise your ethics or spend the bulk of your time with tasks that you find distasteful. It simply means that you have to acknowledge that business considerations are as crucial to your success as the quality of your work. Once you formulate a business policy for yourself, you can hire someone to do part of the work for you, or barter your services with other freelancers who possess the particular business skills you require. But no matter how you go about it, you will effect rapid and positive changes in your career by thinking of yourself as your own business.

Your Own Boss

One of the things that nine-to-fivers often find intriguing is the apparent lack of structure in the lives of those who work for themselves. It is true that freelancers often have a good deal of flexibility in arranging their hours. Unlike nine-to-fivers, freelancers have no clocks to punch and no boss standing over their heads. That is why most veteran freelancers will tell you that self-discipline and the ability to create your own structure are vital keys to success. People who work in a nine-to-five situation know where they have to be and at what time. They also know what their work is and how much they will be paid for that work. In effect, a company's employees are carrying out the business policy of that company. Successful people who work for themselves operate in a similar fashion, but with one important difference: *Employees carry out someone else's business policy while freelancers carry out their own.*

You don't need any special training or expertise to formulate a business policy. Whether you are the owner of a small business, someone in the arts, a housewife, or a salesperson, you can have a business policy that is specifically tailored to your needs. A business policy is nothing more than a clear statement of what you do and how you go about doing it. If you want to increase your earnings and decrease your business-related problems, you can take a giant step in that direction by formulating a specific freelance business policy or improving the one you are currently using. People who run their businesses on a take-it-as-it-comes basis often get paid less than they are worth and wind up spending precious time and energy trying to collect overdue fees. But when you have a specific business policy you get treated with more respect by the people you deal with, and actually wind up spending far less time looking after your businesses.

What Is Your Business Policy?

In order to find out what your current business policy is, write down the answers to as many of the questions in Exercise 1 as you can. Include any plans in your answers that you still have not implemented. If you have never thought about some of the questions, just write "No specific policy" or "I make up a different policy every time." Look over your answers and try to pinpoint those areas that require your special attention.

EXERCISE 1: MY BUSINESS POLICY

1. **What do you do?**   . . . .

2. **What do you call your business?**   . . . .

3. **What are your products and/or services? (Make this
    statement as complete as you can.)**   . . . .

4. **What are your business hours?**   . . . .

5. **Who are your present clients?**   . . . .

6. **Who are your potential clients?**   . . . .

7. **What steps do you take to market and promote your
    work?**   . . . .

8. **What are your pricing guidelines?**   . . . .

9. **How do you negotiate terms?**   . . . .

10. **How do you bill your clients?**   . . . .

11. **Which aspects of your work do you delegate? To
    whom?**   . . . .

12. **What record-keeping systems do you maintain?**   . . . .

13. **What will it cost you to run your business in the
    next year?**   . . . .

14. **What are your projected earnings for the coming
    year?**   . . . .

15. **What are your long-term financial objectives?**   . . . .

16. **Does your budget reflect the cyclical nature of freelance work?**   . . . .

Taking It Step by Step

If you find that your answers to Exercise 1 point to your almost complete lack of any business policy, don't get distressed. It is going to be a lot easier to get your business together than it was to learn the skills you need for your work. Still, you are going to have to direct some positive effort into putting your business policy into shape. Don't try to do everything at once. Pick out something that will be easy to implement and handle that first. For example, if your answer to question 8 was that you had no pricing guidelines, you can take the following steps:

○ Contact experienced people in your field and find out what they charge.

○ Find out if there are any unions, guilds, or other organizations that set pricing guidelines for your kind of work.

○ Try to interview somebody who is familiar with hiring practices in your field and ask them how they determine their freelance rates.

As you go over your answers, pick one area that needs a lot of work and try to make a modest improvement this week. If, for example, you have no system for financial record-keeping, you might want to start out by buying a manila envelope to keep all of your financial records in one place. Freelancers who complete Exercise 1 sometimes feel overwhelmed by all of the work that needs to be done in order to get a business policy into shape. Don't worry. Just take it step by step, and in a relatively short period of time you will see the kind of impact that a well-thought-out business policy can have on your career.

Where to Begin

We asked a number of business persons and financial planners who work with self-employed clients to recommend some basic steps that people can take to improve their business policies. Most of these experts agreed that the handling of finances often creates problems for many freelancers. Here are some simple suggestions that freelancers can use to improve this vital aspect of their businesses.

Keep accurate financial records

Now that you are looking at yourself as a business, it is essential that you keep track of all your business expenses. Get receipts for anything you buy that might be business related. If you are unsure of whether or not a particular expense pertains to your business, get a receipt anyway. If it is inconvenient to ask for a receipt, simply write the expense down in a diary or journal that allows space for you to list your expenses—and write them down as they occur.

Here is a page from the diary of a freelance cameraman. Notice that as he goes through his appointments for the day, he lists all the expenses connected with each appointment:

Set up regular accounts

Another step that you can take to simplify your financial record-keeping is to set up accounts with regular suppliers. Joe, a freelance copywriter who hates to "hassle with things like receipts," set up such an account with his local stationery store. In the past, Joe had regularly purchased pens, typewriter ribbons, and notebooks at the store. Each individual purchase was rather small and the receipts quickly became little balls of paper that crumbled in his pocket. By setting up an account with the stationery store, Joe converted all those little balls of paper into an itemized monthly bill that he filed in a manila envelope marked *stationery supplies*. As an added bonus, the owner of the store gave Joe a 20-percent discount on all purchases. This is a common practice among suppliers who wish to cultivate regular customers.

Hire a qualified accountant

One of the great rewards of keeping accurate financial records comes at tax time. There are a number of tax advantages available to independent contractors; but in order to utilize them properly you will need a qualified accountant who thoroughly understands the nature of your particular business.

Freelance File's Don Reilly is amazed at how many freelancers let themselves get the short end of the financial stick by not employing the right accountant. "You wouldn't go to a brain surgeon for a toothache," he notes. "Why then do some freelancers act so penny wise and dollar foolish by hiring an unqualified accountant or a graduate of some quickie tax preparation course who hasn't got the slightest idea of what freelance businesses are about? The right kind of accountant might cost more money, but you are almost certain to come out ahead if you hire one."

Separate your business and personal finances

As people who are in business for themselves, freelancers should separate their business and personal finances as soon as possible. One of the first steps is to set up two bank accounts: an operating business account and a personal account. All business expenses should be paid for by the operating business account. The canceled checks that come back with your monthly statement become one of your most important hassle-free records. Credit cards should be handled in a similar fashion. Try to use one credit card strictly for your freelance business expenses so that the monthly statements you receive can easily be incorporated into your records.

Self-employed people often remark that their business and personal lives are so intertwined that it is difficult to say which expenses are business and which are personal. Let's say a writer takes an artist friend out to lunch. The chances are that work will be discussed. It is even possible that the conversation will include plans to collaborate on a future project. There certainly is a social aspect to this lunch. However, many business managers and accountants who understand the nature of working for yourself would probably consider that lunch a business expense.

Some people feel that if they are enjoying themselves, then they are not doing business. But business manager David Feinstein disagrees. His vast experience with freelance cameramen, engineers, systems analysts, and rock groups has given him a different point of view on this subject:

"Freelancers should view most of their activities as business related, because this actually is the case more often than not. If you honestly believe that a particular expense is related to your business and you can establish a principle and a point of view for it, you should take the deduction. You are no worse taking a business deduction than not taking it. The worst thing the IRS can do is disallow the deduction and ask you for the tax that would have been due in the first place."

Your own accountant may hold a somewhat less aggressive view on the issue of business deductions. In any case, it is important that all independent contractors understand the delicate relationship between their business and social activities. There is a story about a well-known music business lawyer named Martin that illustrates this fine line: Martin was having a leisurely dinner with a singer who was both his friend and client. When the check came, Martin insisted on paying. "Are you going to write this dinner off as a business expense?" the singer asked. "Certainly," Martin replied. "But does anyone have to know that we *like* talking business?"

Know where your money is going

Do you know where your money is going? We find that many freelancers, some of whom earn very comfortable livings, can't get ahead of their expenses because they have little or no idea of how much money they are spending. Because of the financially uncertain nature of many businesses, it is particularly important that you take a careful look at how you are handling your money. If you insist on spending your money as it comes in, without an overall concept of what you are doing, you might find yourself with some painful financial problems down the road. But if you are willing to take a close look at where your money is going, you will find some relatively painless ways to cut down on your expenses and build a comfortable cushion against future uncertainties.

Chart A (page 14) lists the basic expenses (aside from fixed expenses such as rent, utilities, etc.) that you are likely to incur in any given week. Sit down for a few minutes and try to estimate how much you spend on each item in a typical week. Then take about ten minutes a day and itemize exactly how much you spend on each item that day. Do this for approximately one month and enter your figures on Chart B (page 15).

When you compare the totals of your actual expenses on Chart B to your estimates on Chart A, you should have a pretty good idea of which expenses you can reduce without making any real dent in your lifestyle. You might be surprised to find that you are actually in a position to start saving some money right now.

Chart A: Where Your Money Goes
Estimate of Weekly Expenses

① FOOD	**② EATING OUT**	**③ SUPPLIES & WORK RELATED EXPENSES**
④ ENTERTAINMENT	**⑤ TRANSPORTATION**	**⑥ HOUSEHOLD EXPENSES**
⑦ CHARGE CARD EXPENSES	**⑧ OTHER EXPENSES**	**⑨ TOTAL WEEKLY EXPENSES**

Chart B: Where Your Money Goes
Analysis of Weekly Expenses

Category	Mon	Tues	Wed	Thu	Fri	Sat	Sun	Total
① FOOD								
② EATING OUT Breakfast Lunch Dinner								
③ SUPPLIES & WORK RELATED EXPENSES								
④ ENTERTAINMENT								
⑤ TRANSPORTATION								
⑥ HOUSEHOLD EXPENSES								
⑦ CHARGE CARD EXPENSES								
⑧ OTHER EXPENSES								
⑨ TOTAL WEEKLY EXPENSES								

© P. Namanworth & G. Busner 1982

Set up a program of systematic savings

Some freelancers might feel that it is premature to concern themselves with savings when they are still struggling to pay last month's rent. But financial planners who specialize in self-employed clients feel that it is never too soon to begin the habit of channeling small amounts of money into savings. Erna Ferris is a financial advisor who deals primarily with the self-employed. Here is how she poses the issue of savings to her clients:

15

"You have to weigh certain comforts against financial security in the future. If you are willing to cut down on things like taxis and eating out, you can channel that $20 or $25 a week into a savings account. It really doesn't matter where you put your money or how much interest it is earning. The most important thing is that you save money on a consistent, systematic basis."

A systematic savings program is particularly important for anyone who is subject to a cyclical income. The person who earns $5,000 one month and no money for the next six months would be well advised not to act as if he or she is earning $60,000 a year. Erna Ferris has the following suggestions for those who must deal with a cyclical or inconsistent income:

"If you earn a good deal of money one month but no money, say, for the next six months, it might be a good idea to take care of your rent, utilities and other fixed expenses for that entire period. Then, if you make more money than you anticipated, you can spend part of it on comforts and put the rest of it into savings."

Saving money shows that you are concerned with taking care of the future. If you are the type of person who would rather live day-to-day and take each tomorrow as a new challenge, you do so at your own risk. Unfortunately, this kind of attitude often leads to trouble. Working for yourself has enough built-in uncertainty as it is. As a successful freelancer you must devote part of your time and energy to avoiding problems that are likely to arise down the road. If you don't take care of tomorrow, nobody else is going to do it for you.

Principle 2:
YOU CAN OVERCOME OBSTACLES BY EFFECTIVE PLANNING

MANY OF THE PROBLEMS THAT FREELANCERS MOST often complain about stem from a lack of effective planning. Just as you need a business policy, you also require some kind of overall plan that lends a sense of order and structure to your lives in general. Once you formulate a plan and commit yourself to it, you have made a major decision that can save you the anxiety of dealing with a hundred smaller decisions every day.

I Hate Mondays

Self-employed people who don't plan effectively often complain about what we call the I-hate-Mondays syndrome. The nine-to-fiver might curse and grunt when the alarm goes off on Monday morning, but he drags himself out of bed because he has to arrive at his job on time and ready for work. Freelancers, especially those who work at home, also curse and grunt when the alarm goes off. But since the nature of independent work often does not include the pressure to get to work at any particular hour, people are tempted to turn off the alarm and go back to sleep. Some find it hard to face the uncertainty that each new day brings, the deadlines that they will never meet, and the vague goals that they never seem to get started on. This type

17

Positive thinking

of person often winds up saying, "To hell with Monday. I'll get rolling tomorrow." One actress described her feelings about Monday as follows:

> "It's Sunday evening. I've had a nice restful weekend— done a few things, taken in a movie and enjoyed myself. Slowly, a creeping sense of anxiety sets in. It's Sunday night; tomorrow is Monday. Tomorrow it all starts again—the uncertainty; the time on my hands; the work I can't get myself to do; the haphazardness of it all. Oh, how I wish the weekend would last forever. *I hate Mondays.*"

By planning effectively, you can avoid this sense of anxiety and frustration. There's nothing wrong with hating Mondays. Unfortunately, these kinds of feelings tend to carry over to Tuesday and all the other days of the week. People who procrastinate know that they need better self-discipline. But this has little meaning for people who have nothing to discipline themselves for. That is why it's so important to set definite objectives and work them into a systematic overall plan.

The Myth of Having Nothing to Do

No matter how hard some people may fight it, there is *always* something worthwhile to do. Even if there is no work coming in, you can be out there generating new clients. And what about that sloppy desk that you've been thinking about straightening out, or that two-year-old project you've been wanting to revise? Freelancers who plan effectively find that there is always work to do. So the next time you think that there is nothing to do, ask yourself if any of the following requires your attention:

1. Planning short- and long-range strategies

2. Reading trade publications and other relevant materials

3. Developing and implementing personal marketing techniques

4. Developing new projects

5. Revising older projects

6. Completing work already assigned

7. Making business contacts

8. Procuring work via meetings, letters, and phone calls

9. Improving workspace

10. Follow-up

Once you accept all the responsibilities that your career entails, you can always find something to do to improve your present situation or enhance your future prospects. Commit yourself to a well-thought-out plan, and you can overcome almost any obstacle in your work. Here are two cases in point:

The organized slob

Ira is a highly regarded freelance writer in the electronics field. Before we went to interview him at his home/office we were warned that he was a formidable slob. These reports were not exaggerated. Ira's living room was littered with books, papers, records, and sandwich wrappers. But in spite of this seemingly total chaos, for which he freely admitted responsibility, Ira claimed that he could locate any piece of work-related material within seconds:

> "I know I'm a terrible slob, but I've been forced to overcome that in my work. . . . Many of the articles that I write can be sold to a number of publications with only minor revisions. That means I've got to be able to put my hands on information in a hurry. Being a slob is a personal weakness or problem, however you want to look at it. I probably won't be able to correct it in my personal life and I'm not sure I really want to. But I realized a long time ago that if I was going to be a successful freelance writer, I would have to overcome my natural sloppiness and lack of organization.
>
> The way I do this is to impose all kinds of organizational systems on myself. Obviously, I need a lot of help

"Who took my appointment calendar from under the bologna sandwich?"

21

with this aspect of my work. That's why I've made it part of my planning to have a secretary come in twice a week to organize my files. This creates a rather large expense for me, especially when there isn't a lot of work coming in. But I could never make a living if I didn't plan to have that kind of help."

Before we left Ira's office, we mentioned that we were looking for a certain kind of gadget that would allow us to record telephone interviews. In no more than thirty seconds, Ira made his way through the rubble on the floor, opened one of his files, and told us the model number and price of the gadget.

Fear of phoning

A sales representative named Sue had a problem with phone calls. She had no trouble calling up new clients for appointments, but she got frazzled when they didn't return her calls immediately. "It was really strange," she said. "I always had this sinking feeling that people weren't ever going to call me back. This would make me very anxious and unable to work."

Sue eventually realized that the root of her difficulty was a lack of planning. She was putting too much emphasis on the phone calls instead of viewing them as only one part of her work. "I finally came to realize that the real problem wasn't the phone calls. It was just a result of poor planning and not having my time structured properly." These days, Sue makes phone calls at certain planned times during the week and then moves on to some other aspect of her work. "I feel so much better now that I look at calling clients as number five on my to-do list," she says. "Instead of waiting for people to call me back and worrying about it, I just take care of the next thing I have scheduled for that day."

Here is a page from Sue's diary. By scheduling a number of work-related activities for that day, Sue minimizes the time spent worrying about clients calling her back:

Friday, May 28

Things to do:

1. Review client list
2. Pick samples for 2PM meeting
3. Send invoice to XYZ
4. Pick up Biz. Cards

5. CALLS
   A Dabney's Meeting (?)
   B Smith (Overdue bill)
   C. Joann's (New Client)

6 Work on proposal (Tiffany Inc.)

Time	Appointments/Events	Follow-up/Remarks	($)
10:00 AM	Ro-Mart Stationery	Cancelled - call to reschedule	
12:00 PM	Accountant (Joe Cohen) 12 W. 35 St.	Check 1981 bank statements	cab $3.60
2:00 PM	Jones Meeting 316 Madison Ave Suite 2A	Call next Tues.	cab $4.65
3:00 PM	Lee Shop (bring samples)	Meeting on Mon. 5/31 10 AM	
6:00 PM	Dinner - w/client (Maxwell)	Put together proposal call in app. 2 weeks	Luna Rest $38.70

Bright Ideas

Put Maxwell in touch with XYZ

No matter what kinds of obstacles prevent you from getting your work done, effective planning is the key to overcoming them. The structure provided by schedules and to-do lists can help you work better. However, many people tend to ignore their schedules when they are created without the context of an overall plan. (In Chapter Six, which deals with using time effectively, we will fully explore the techniques of planning a schedule that is right for you.) If the activities that fill our days are to have any meaning, they must be linked to the achievement of specific goals we have set for ourselves. With this in mind, we turn our attention to charting the course that leads to those goals.

Principle 3:
YOU DETERMINE YOUR OWN SUCCESS

We make our own fortunes and we call them fate.
Disraeli

SINCE WE ARE DISCUSSING THE INGREDIENTS FOR successful self-employment, let's take a moment to reflect on the meaning of *success*. Everybody wants to be successful. But what does that mean? Many people in our society measure success in dollars or the material things that money can buy. Others long for the power and status that come from being at the top of a particular field. Since people who work for themselves are so diverse in their lifestyles, they sometimes think of success in less conventional terms. Some have very modest aspirations in terms of money and power. They would be quite happy to make just enough to make ends meet—if only they could work on their own terms. Others want their lifestyles to include three or four months a year for leisure and travel.

As we see it, success means achieving the goals that you have set for yourself. No matter what your goals are, you are more likely to achieve them if they reflect your own hopes and dreams rather than those of society, your family or anyone else. The following is a four-step process designed to help you achieve your own particular goals in the shortest time possible.

• *Define success for yourself.* What does success mean to you? Write down a few long-range goals. Don't worry if some of your goals seem farfetched. After all, these are your hopes and dreams and, for the moment, they should have a free rein. As we have noted, some general categories for success might include money, power, travel, leisure, and achievement in your work. You can use these categories as guidelines, but do not limit your answers to them. Ask yourself the following questions: What kinds of things do I really want for myself? Are there things that I tend to overlook because I am afraid that they are too unconventional or unattainable?

• *Be specific about your goals.* After you've written down your general definition for success, try to be more specific. Instead of simply saying, "I want to make a lot of money," say, "I want to make $100,000 a year." Instead of merely stating a desire to travel for three months a year, say, "I want to spend every winter on a tropical beach." If one of your definitions for success involves recognition in your work, state that goal in terms of a specific award or other recognizable achievement. As time goes by, you can alter your goals and the criteria for meeting them.

• *Write down what has to be done to achieve each of your goals.* When you establish a goal, it is essential that you take a look at the work you will need to do to reach that goal. Let's say one of your goals is to have a best-selling novel. There are plenty of people, including nonwriters, who would love to have the money and glory of a best-seller. But how many are willing to do the work that is needed to get to that point? It can take years to write a novel. And this is only the beginning. The finished work has to be sold to a publisher, edited, and publicized correctly once it gets on the market. So your goal of having a best-selling novel would contain the following major steps:

1. Conceive of an idea for the book.

2. Write a first draft.

3. Make the necessary revisions.

4. Find a publisher or an agent to represent you.

5. Negotiate a deal that assures that you receive your proper share (this might entail hiring a lawyer).

6. Make further revisions in the book as per your publisher's request.

7. Make public appearances to promote the book once it comes out.

Each of these steps can be broken down even further. For example, you might want to read over some of your old notes and short stories before you settle on the idea you are going to pursue. To this end, your goal of writing a best-seller would express itself by devoting three hours on Tuesday to going over notes and ideas. And this is an important key in achieving success on your own terms: *Your long-range goals must be broken down into manageable steps that you can implement on a daily and weekly basis.* It is the completion of many small and related steps that ultimately gets you to where you want to go.

• *Set deadlines for your goals.* In order to plan effectively, it is important that you conceive of your goals within a time framework. If you decide that it is going to take two years to create a best-seller, you can start planning your work schedule around that goal. The deadlines you establish should be flexible enough to allow for unforeseen delays. If you find that you are constantly moving your deadlines ahead, you might want to question how realistic they are. Try to consider the length of time it will take to achieve all of the plateaus and steps that lead to your long-range goal. Be sure to set some intermediate deadlines for each plateau. If you add all of those together, you should get a general idea of how long the project will take. We find that it is better to set approximate deadlines than to work without them completely. All of our lives are governed and limited by time. It is a variable that must be considered in setting any kind of realistic goals.

The Process in Action

To get a better understanding of how the process of achieving success can work for you, let's look at a portion of an interview we conducted with a freelancer named Frank. When Frank first came to see us, he was very unfocused in his goals. "I want to make a lot of money," Frank answered when we asked how he defined success. "What are you going to do to make this money?" we asked. "Well," said Frank, "I've been a singer most of my life, but I'm thinking about getting into acting. I also have a friend in the jewelry business who wants me to get involved with that." After narrowing down the goals that he felt most strongly about, Frank concluded that his primary desire was to become a successful singer/songwriter. Here is how we helped Frank break that long-range goal down into plateaus and, finally, into groups that he could begin to implement immediately:

Q: How would you define achieving success as a songwriter?
A: Having my own album out.

Q: What would that entail?

A: Getting signed by a record company.

Q: How does this happen?

A: You bring them your tapes and see if they like them.

Q: Good. Are you going to bring them tapes?

A: Well, not exactly. I still haven't made any tapes.

Q: What do you have to do to make the tapes?

A: I've got to find a musical arranger and some musicians to play my songs.

Q: Have you done that?

A: Not really.

Q: How come?

A: Well, I haven't really finished the songs yet, although I do have parts of two of them pretty well worked out.

Q: Why don't you start out by finishing the song that is closest to completion. Which one is that?

A: It's called, "I Love You, Baby."

Q: So the first plateau in reaching your goal is to finish "I Love You Baby." What needs to get done next?

A: I've got to write down the music in a legible, professional way.

Q: What is that called?

A: A lead sheet.

Q: Can you do that yourself?

A: No, I need to hire a professional copyist to do a lead sheet.

Q: So, the second plateau in reaching your goal is to get the lead sheet done. What would you have to do next?

A: I need an arranger to write the parts down for the musicians.

Q: Do you know any arrangers?

A: I know three arrangers who might be right, but I'll have to talk to them first.

Q: Fine. Your third plateau would be to find an arranger. Then what?

A: Well, the arranger will hire the musicians, but I don't have the money right now for the musicians or the recording studio.

Q: How much will that cost?

A: I don't know exactly, but I could find out.

Q: Let's call that your fourth plateau: Set up a budget for musicians and studio costs. Do you think you will be able to raise the money?

A: I think so. But it might take a while.

Q: That's okay. Your fifth plateau is to raise the money for the project. What comes next?

A: Well, I go in and finish my tape. I guess that's the sixth plateau in reaching my goal.

Q: Right. This seems like an important stage in your project. How will you go about getting your tape to a record company?

A: I could take it myself, but I think it's better to find an agent or a manager.

Q: Good. That's the seventh plateau. What else needs to get done?

A: The agent or manager takes the tape into a record company. If they like it, they make an offer. At that point, I'll probably need a lawyer.

Q: Then the eighth plateau is to find a music business lawyer. Then what happens?

A: He negotiates a deal and I make a record.

Let's summarize what we have found out about Frank. We established that one of his primary long-range goals was to get a recording contract as a singer/songwriter. We then worked our way through the eight plateaus that Frank would need to reach before he achieves that goal. Each one of these plateaus has to be broken down even further into manageable steps so that Frank can deal with them on a daily and weekly basis. Each step that Frank takes may not seem terribly significant. But because Frank understands that each time he completes a step, he gets a little closer to his goal, it is easier for him to sustain his motivation and stick with the process through the various steps and plateaus until he finally reaches his long-range goal.

Here then is a chart that diagrams the steps that Frank will have to climb in order to achieve his goal:

LONG-RANGE GOAL: To become a successful singer/songwriter

Specific Criterion: Be signed as a recording artist to a record company
Deadline: one year from today

Plateaus

I. Finish songs.
    Deadline: two months

    a. Set up a file to keep all relevant information.
    b. Complete "I Love You, Baby."
    c. Look through batch of uncompleted songs.
    d. Pick three others (already started) to complete.
    e. Complete first song by two weeks.
    f. Complete second song by five weeks.
    g. Complete third song by eight weeks.

II. **Get lead sheets done.**
Deadline: one month

    a. Call Don to get names of copyists.
    b. Call three; ask to see samples; get prices.
    c. Research other sources for copyists.
    d. Select a copyist to do the lead sheets.

III. **Find an arranger.**
Deadline: two months

    a. Get names of arrangers from Sheila.
    b. Find out who arranged some records I like; try to reach them.
    c. Pick two arrangers and meet with them. Discuss price and work.
    d. Select one.
    e. Go over finished arrangement. Make any necessary changes.

IV. **Set up a budget.**
Deadline: two months

    a. Find out cost of lead sheets.
    b. Find out cost of arranger.
    c. Find out cost of recording studio, including tape copies.
    d. Find out cost of musicians and instrument rentals.
    e. Estimate total plus a 10 percent leeway.

V. **Raise money to cover costs of musicians and recording studio.**
Deadline: one month

    a. Do self-study to see if I can save more money to achieve this goal.

    b. Estimate savings and cash availability.

    c. Try to barter for some of the services I require.

    d. Look into borrowing from credit union and/or other sources.

VI. **Finish making tape.**
Deadline: one month

    a. Hire musicians.

    b. Book studio time at XYZ Studio (try to book off-hours for better rate).

    c. Record instrumental and vocal tracks.

    d. Mix tape.

    e. Make tape copies to send out.

VII. **Find a manager or agent.**
Deadline: one month

    a. Check list of managers or agents I know.

    b. Call friends for names of their contacts.

    c. Check trade magazines for names.

    d. Select four possibilities.

    e. Call and see them with tape.

    f. Select one to represent me.

VIII. **Hire a music business lawyer.**
Deadline: one month

    a. Get names of three lawyers.

    b. Go see them to talk generally (for free if possible).

    c. Select one on the basis of reputation and effectiveness.

Proceed With Confidence

Now that you see how the process of achieving success and defining goals works, pick one or more of your own goals and break them down—first into plateaus and then into manageable steps.

Remember: you can set any pace for accomplishing whatever goals you choose. However, you may find that your original deadline was unrealistic and needs to be revised. In any case, you will need perseverance and a degree of luck to achieve your long-range goals. By utilizing the principles we have outlined in this chapter, you will maximize your chances for success in any field.

To help you, we've provided an outline for you to work with to begin the process *today*.

LONG-RANGE GOAL:

Specific Criterion:
Deadline:

Plateaus

I.

Deadline:

a.

b.

c.

d.

e.

f.

g.

II.

Deadline:

a.

b.

c.

d.

e.

f.

g.

III.

Deadline:

a.

b.

c.

d.

e.

f.

g.

IV.

Deadline:

a.

b.

c.

d.

e.

f.

g.

V.

Deadline:

a.

b.

c.

d.

e.

f.

g.

VI.

Deadline:

a.

b.

c.

d.

e.

f.

g.

VII.

Deadline:

a.

b.

c.

d.

e.

f.

g.

2

The Individual Business Structure (IBS) or . . . How to Run the Most Important Business on This Planet—YOURS!!!

TEN COMMON COMPLAINTS

PEOPLE WHO WORK FOR THEMSELVES FREQUENTLY voice many of the same complaints about running their businesses. Do any of the following sound familiar to you?

☺ I can't get organized.

☺ I don't like to sell myself.

☺ I'm always putting things off until the last minute.

☺ I'm bad at dealing with money.

☺ I'm a lousy negotiator.

☺ I feel isolated working alone.

☺ I can't get going in the morning.

☺ I'm not good at following through.

☺ I get anxious when I'm between projects.

☺ I can't structure my day.

How do successful people overcome these nagging problems? There has been much written on the specific techniques of getting organized, setting up a budget, negotiating, etc. (Thumb through the pages of this book and you will find lots of information and tips on how to handle particular difficulties.) But most of us require more than cold facts to handle troublesome areas. We need an overall context to put day-to-day problems in the right perspective, a sense of structure that begins to take shape the moment we make a commitment to handling our careers according to the principles that govern all successful businesses.

YOURS IS THE MOST IMPORTANT BUSINESS ON THIS PLANET!!!

IF YOU'VE EVER OBSERVED PEOPLE WHO OWN their own businesses you know that they are not above sweeping the floor, making deliveries, or doing anything else it might take

to keep their companies running. You need to look at yourselves in the same light. Not only are you chief executive officer of your company, you also handle most of the chores, be they creative, clerical, or janitorial. If you were an employee of someone else's company you would probably have a defined role in that organization. But when you work for yourself, you are not merely an employee—in a very real sense you *are* the company. Once you develop this kind of perspective on your work, you take a crucial step towards becoming successful freelancer.

Jill, a script writer, had been doing well for several years. Yet until very recently she went about her daily tasks without any real sense of direction. She recalls:

"I used to think of myself as this insignificant little freelance writer who worked out of her apartment and was lucky to pay the bills. But I realized that the decisions I make in my business have more impact on my success than any single decision a giant corporation might make. A large company can fire the people who screw up, but I can't very well fire myself. After years of basically living from day to day, I began to look at what successful companies do and tried to follow their lead. Now, I don't take a back seat to anybody because I genuinely believe that in many ways, my business is more important than General Motors or IBM. After all, can anyone else's business have more of an impact on my success?"

YOUR INDIVIDUAL BUSINESS STRUCTURE (IBS)

IF YOU WERE THE PRESIDENT OF A LARGE CORPOration, you would hire:

decision makers to formulate the company's objectives

managers to translate these objectives into concrete plans, and
workers to execute the specific actions.

As a self-employed person, you are going to have to assume these functions yourself. Does that sound like a lot of work? It is. But do you know successful people in any business who achieve

THE THREE STAGES OF YOUR IBS

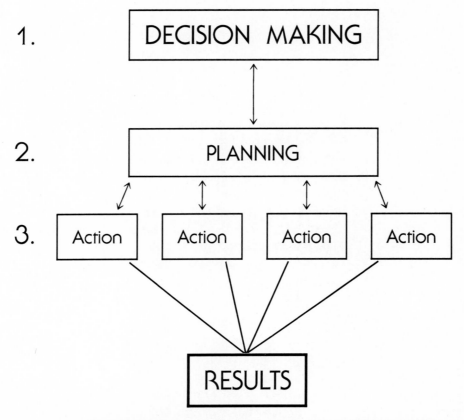

THE INDIVIDUAL BUSINESS STRUCTURE: A DYNAMIC PROCESS

their objectives without hard work? Not to worry: You won't have to work three times as hard. In fact, once you understand which level you're operating on—and when—you'll find yourself accomplishing more in far less time.

The best way to understand the three levels of your Individual Business Structure is to imagine that you are wearing one of three hats as you transact your business.

Decision Making:
You are the Chief Executive

If you were about to embark on a brand new business venture, it would be prudent to sit down and make some basic decisions about the nature of your business and the objectives you'd wish to achieve. Unfortunately, some people never take this essential first step in creating a workable structure for themselves. As a result, they have all kinds of day-to-day problems that severely limit their success. Most of us can point to a friend or acquaintance (or ourselves) and note that he or she seems to get by quite nicely without any apparent structure. Usually, such individuals have developed some kind of personal method that roughly parallels the kind of structure we are expounding, or they are highly skilled people whose work is in great demand. In both cases, the implementation of a specifically formulated, custom-designed structure would do much to create a climate for greater success. Whether you're just launching a new career or have been working in the same field for many years, you will profit immeasurably by carefully considering the aims and objectives of your business.

Can you succeed without deciding what your business objectives are? Maybe. But you will probably have to do a lot of unnecessary work and put yourself through a good deal of emotional stress. The lives of self-employed people are filled with enough uncertainties without frantic activity. As we see it, anyone who operates without such objectives is like a chicken without a head. Nine-to-fivers generally will get fired if they go around like chickens without heads because their bosses have hired them to carry out company objectives that have already been formulated. Since you are your own boss, it's up to you to decide what your objectives are.

Put on your executive hat

Pick an hour or two when things are calm: Use this time to decide your business objectives. Do not think of yourself as Joe Smith, a puny little freelancer who is trying to keep one step ahead of his bills. Instead, think of yourself as the *Executive Officer* of the Joe Smith Organization. Forget your day-to-day hassles for now and project yourself into the future, keeping in mind that it is this kind of thinking that underlies every successful business. Take a few minutes to complete the following exercise:

DECISION MAKING

☐ In one or two short paragraphs, state the aims of your business.

☐ List your five most important goals in order of priority and state when you would like to achieve them by.

☐ Select the two goals that would be easiest for you to implement.

Congratulations! You have taken a significant step in creating the kind of business structure that provides a framework for success. By putting on your executive hat, you have removed yourself from the daily problems that taunt you and set the stage for positive action that will help clear them up. Before you get down to your daily work, though, you need to map out the road you will take in order to achieve your objectives.

Planning:
What You Need to Know

One of the things that businesses often do after they formulate their policies and objectives is to determine how these are to be implemented. Let's pretend for a moment that you are an outside consultant and that you've been brought in to turn the decisions that were made on an executive level into specific plans. Your primary role as a planner is to break down goals into plans, which bring results through actions. A plan is very much like a road map, and you are the traveler. It's great to have a destination, but unless you have a map to guide you there, you're not likely to get very far.

Put on your planning hat

In Chapter One, we showed how goals can be broken down into plateaus, steps, and substeps. If you are working with a goal that is familiar, you probably understand something about what it takes to get there. But what if the goal is unfamiliar? Chances are you will have to spend a good deal of time gathering relevant data. In either case, you need all kinds of information to be effective planners. When you put on your planning hat, you will want to have the following kinds of data at your fingertips:

WHAT YOU NEED TO BE AN EFFECTIVE PLANNER

 A knowledge of how your business works

 An understanding of the marketplace

 An understanding of the specific tasks needed to complete your goal

 Information about external conditions that may affect you

 An understanding of what obstacles you are likely to encounter

 A knowledge of how fast you work

 A familiarity with people and services you may require

 A knowledge of how to go about getting the information you lack

You are going to invest some time gathering the information that will turn you into an effective planner, but it is an investment which pays high dividends. Time-efficiency expert Robert Moskowitz calls planning "the mechanism that lets you get out of the crush and constant flow of events. . . . Good planning puts you in the driver's seat instead of under the rear wheels."[1]

You don't need any special talents to become an effective planner. All you require is a desire to improve your business and the willingness to take the necessary steps that make your desire a reality. After you have gathered all the necessary data that pertains to a particular goal, you are ready to map out the plateaus and steps that will get you where you want to go. Here are some questions to consider when mapping out your plan:

> ▶ Where am I now in relation to my goal?
>
> ▶ Based on my data, do my priorities established in decision making still stand?
>
> ▶ What is the best place for me to start?
>
> ▶ Is there more than one way for me to reach my destination?
>
> ▶ Which available route is best for me?

When should you plan?

Since planning is at the center of this three-tiered process, your effectiveness at this stage is vital. One mistake that freelancers sometimes make is to plan while they are caught up in the events of their work day. We find that the best plans are formulated when people are calm and fully able to concentrate. The end of your work day or the morning, before your work day begins, are good times for planning. Ideally, your plan allows you to create an agenda to which you will adhere. So if you want to minimize anxiety, gain more control over your life, and ultimately achieve your goals, take the time and effort to plan properly. It will pay off!

Action! Making It Happen

What do you know? It's Monday morning again and another new week is about to begin. You've got a clearer picture of your career than you ever thought possible because you've taken the time to set up the first two stages of your Individual Business Structure. But the peace and quiet that pervaded policy making and planning seem far away now. That overdue assignment is still sitting on your desk along with last month's unpaid bills. You've got to go to the bank and the post office, and on top of that, you've been barraged with personal calls all morning.

Welcome to the action stage! This is crucible of your Individual Business Structure—the place where everything comes out in the proverbial wash. This is the level where self-employed people voice complaints like "I can't get organized," "I can't get going in the morning," "I hate making calls," and so on.

Jamie, a freelance architect, always had problems keeping his files in order. After working through the first two stages of his IBS, he realized that maintaining an orderly filing system was essential to reach his goal of doubling his client base in the next year. "It's funny," Jamie recalls, "a friend happened to drop by a few days ago while I was reordering my files. He said, 'God, you've really changed; the last thing I expected to see was you hassling with your filing system.' Truthfully, I'm still not crazy about filing, but I understand that it's something that has to get done if I'm ever going to realize my objectives."

Put on your action hat

The best way to visualize yourself at the action level is as a worker. Pretend for a moment that you were hired by someone else to spend the next three hours typing letters. You wouldn't question the rightness of your boss's decision to have those letters typed, would you? You might ask if something had been left out or if the form of the letter was suitable, but you certainly wouldn't tell your employer that you weren't in the mood or you didn't think he was running his business properly. As your own boss, you have a lot more flexibility, but you would do well to carry out the tasks that you have set for yourself in Planning with

The freelancer's pink slip

at least the same dedication you would expect of an employee. All businesses hire workers to carry out their policies and plans, and yours is no different—even if it is you who does most of the carrying out. It's great to establish objectives and map out appropriate routes, but unless you take the necessary actions you are a lot like the guy who decides to take a trip, obtains all the necessary information and then proceeds to fall asleep at the wheel.

Action Gives Life to Goals

Actions take on new meaning if they connect with the rest of your IBS. Whenever you're faced with a task that causes you to ask the question "Why do I have to do this?"—the

John Smith: man of action

answer can be found by reviewing decision making and planning. Successful people make it their business to follow through at the action level; they do not let self-doubt prevent them from getting their work done. When you do the work you've set for yourself, you reinforce your commitment to your business and strengthen the habit of following through.

Remember: you've already given careful consideration to your goals and plans, so don't rethink them every day; stick to them for a long enough period of time to see if they are working out for you. We find that freelancers often abandon their plans too soon. If the road gets rough, don't stop driving. Figure out an alternate route to get where you want to go. Here are some useful tools to help you function on the action level:

ACTION

☞ **Make a daily agenda based on the activities needed to carry out your plans.**

☞ **Consider your deadlines.**

☞ **Reflect deadlines in your daily schedule.**

☞ **Pick five priorities to start with.**

☞ **Cross off each task upon completion.**

☞ **If you complete your priorities early enough, add three more.**

Make a "Did" list

Write down tasks you've completed along with any follow-up information. Acknowledging your completion of tasks will help you avoid frustration and provide you with a way of measuring results. When you've completed a particular goal-related action, you are ready to add the next one to your agenda, according to your plan. In this way, you stay in touch with the progress you are making in reaching your goal.

Review

At the end of one month, review your accomplishments. Take note of the progress you've made. You may want to do this weekly. Also note the tasks you've been putting off. Problems rooted at the action level usually come about for three major reasons: you hate the task; or you have the task scheduled at the wrong time of the day for you; or you think doing the task has further implications that overwhelm you.

The Individual Business Structure

The Individual Business Structure is an ongoing process that gives self-employed people a structure in which to work, learn, and become successful. As you will see, the principles of the Individual Business Structure apply to all aspects of your functioning, be they financial, organizational, or lifestyle. Like any process, the IBS isn't foolproof. We cannot guarantee that everyone will achieve their objectives by following the IBS. For example, you aren't going to "make it" as a classical musician if you don't have a great deal of talent, no matter what you do. You're also not likely to sell a lot of thermal underwear in a city where the temperature rarely falls below 80 degrees. However, you will greatly increase your chances for success by utilizing the

IBS, and you will develop important habits for successful self-employment.

The IBS is a logical process; as such it can help you locate problems within its system. If, for example, you set an unrealistic goal, you may not realize it until you are well into the action stage.

Dave, a computer programmer with three years' experience, decided to leave his full-time position and become a consultant. He saved enough money to quit his job and launch his own business. Dave had acquired a good deal of information about how to start his new company and his new plans were mapped out with great care. His financial goal was to earn $30,000 the first year and $50,000 the second year. However, as the first year progressed, he realized that he needed to spend so much time making contacts and lining up clients that he had very little time left to handle the work he was able to generate. He also found that many clients wouldn't need his services for six months to a year. When he sat down to evaluate his results at the end of the first year, he had only earned $12,000. Dave realized his problem stemmed from mistaking a short-term goal for a long-term goal. He had succeeded in getting his new business off the ground and simply needed to restructure the time frame for his financial goal. He reset his second year goal for $20,000, his third year for $35,000 and his fourth year goal for $50,000, realizing that further revision might be necessary, depending on business conditions.

Another common problem comes from an oversight during the planning stage. Barbara, a talented popular vocalist who had done some advertising work over the last few years, decided that she wanted to increase her income by getting work as a lead singer on commercials. She put together a tape of her best work and sent it around to as many people as she could identify as potential employers. No response. There were two problems in Barbara's plan. First of all, she did not realize that most work in this field was obtained through establishing a network of contracts. Furthermore, at the time there was little demand for lead singers relative to background singers. Once she was able to obtain these two vital pieces of information, Barbara reevaluated her plans and eventually had more success in finding work singing commercials.

Problems that occur on the action level are the ones we most often hear about. In fact, people without an Individual Business Structure often function only on the action level. If you've taken care in formulating decisions and plans, the action level should be straightforward enough. Theoretically, as a worker at the action level, you simply carry out the tasks presented to you by planning. But fortunately (or unfortunately, depending on how you look at it), we are not robots. Sometimes there are things that we need to get done in order to achieve our objectives that we simply will not do.

Greg, a freelance graphic designer, could not bring himself to deal with his finances. He had established the need to get his finances in order during the decision-making stage and designated time slots for related tasks on his agenda. Still, he just wouldn't pay his outstanding bills (though he had more than enough money to cover them). Not only that, he couldn't muster the energy to bill clients for fees on projects he had completed. "For a long time," Greg admits, "I just figured I'd be able to get by never having to deal with finances. But once I decided to look at my work in a more businesslike way, I saw that I was never going to progress until I found some way to take care of my financial situation. The solution for me was to pay somebody to handle this aspect of my life. I now have a business manager who gets a small percentage of my income, and he handles every detail of my financial life. Not only do I have more cash and a growing savings account, I have more time and energy for those things I am really interested in doing."

PULLING IT ALL TOGETHER

THE INDIVIDUAL BUSINESS STRUCTURE IS A DY-
namic process, not a rigid set of rules. The three levels feed into
each other and there is a degree of overlap in how they operate.
Utilizing the IBS will help you make more money, have more
free time for yourself, and achieve more of your long-range
objectives than those who operate in a haphazard, unstructured
way.

Working for yourself holds unlimited potential if you can
maximize the advantages. Anyone who is in business for himself
or herself must be ready to accept a great deal of responsibility.
Financial advisor and radio personality Bill Bresnan—a highly
successful freelancer himself—feels that a key concept for self-
employed people to grasp is that . . . "they must account for
themselves . . . that's the hardest kind of responsibility because
you're looking in the mirror. Instead of going through committees
and buffers that are built into corporate bureaucracies, freelancers must face everything themselves."

When you set up an IBS, you confirm your commitment to
do whatever it takes to succeed. When you work for yourself,
you need this kind of self-created structure. People often have a
difficult time getting things done on their own, yet numerous
studies show that when self-motivation takes effect, it becomes a
more inspiring force than any boss could ever be.

So when you feel overwhelmed, remember that working for
yourself is not necessarily the easiest road to take. But, as Bill
Bresnan points out, "Self-employment can have very positive
long-term results. If you're successful at it, you'll be much better
off than employees in the corporate sphere."

Review of the Three Levels of the IBS

I. Decision Making:

    a.   Set goals and priorities.

    b.   Review progress and evaluate results.

II. Planning:

    a.   Gather information.

    b.   Map out routes.

III. Action:

    a.   Carry out tasks.

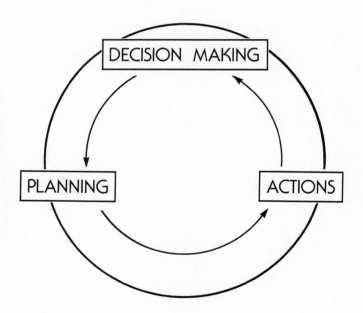

3

GAINING
FINANCIAL CONTROL:
Dealing with Money Is a
Pain . . .
But Not Having It Is Worse

"Dealing with money is a big pain in the ass," an architect named Jack groaned over a recent lunch. "I'm making more money now than I ever did before, but my financial situation seems to be getting worse: I'm overextended on all my credit cards; my studio was recently burglarized of thousands of dollars worth of equipment that I never got around to insuring; the IRS is auditing me for the last three years and I'm really sweating because I didn't bother keeping any receipts or records. I've got to say it again: Dealing with money is one big pain in the ass."

Why do so many freelancers feel the way Jack does about money? For one thing, they've never been given the tools to deal with it. That required course in economics did little more than prove to most of us that the world of finance was an endless fountain of complicated and boring terms with no relevance to our lives or anyone else's. And it's not just people in the arts who can't get their finances together. We've met a surprising number of M.B.A.'s who make their living giving financial advice but who have problems balancing their own checkbooks. We were recently talking with the chairman of the business department of a major college about teaching a course at his institution. "I'm going to make it a point to audit your class," he told us. "My finances are a mess and I don't have the vaguest notion of how to create a realistic budget for myself."

Let's face it: Setting up budgets and financial records aren't among the enticing activities in most of our lives. "Most people find money a boring—and scary—subject, and they choose to avoid it," says financial author and radio personality Bernard Meltzer. "Even if you're a finance major in college," he adds, "you learn about money from the theoretical, not the practical side. If you study accounting, you learn about it from a technical point of view."

We can't disagree with Meltzer's analysis of the widespread lack of practical financial knowledge among people in all walks of life. Still, we know from hard experience that when you don't take control of your money, your money winds up controlling you.

An analogy we like to use for investing a little time and energy in taking financial control relates to the similarities between physical and financial health. People in good physical shape usually invest a few hours a week in some program of regular exercise. It's not that they necessarily think that sit-ups and push-ups are more fun than sitting around watching television. Those who devote time to exercise are rewarded in the short run by more attractive bodies, and in the long run by better physical health. With financial health, the same principles apply. If you put a little bit of time each week into keeping your money matters together, you will ultimately spend a lot less time curing financial ills.

CLEARING UP THE GREAT MONEY MYSTERY

THERE IS AN ATTITUDE ABOUT MONEY THAT WE'D like to clear up right now, and that is the notion that only accountants, bankers, and other supposed mavens are capable of grasping the essentials of your financial life. It's not only your reticence or lack of training that makes you back off from dealing with money, but a conscious effort by some financial institutions that hope to profit by keeping you in the dark. Here's what the noted economist John Kenneth Galbraith has to say on this matter: "It is especially important that no one be put off by the fraudulent air of mystery that surrounds all questions having to do with banks and money."[1]

As you will see, most financial concepts can be explained in everyday terms that relate to your particular needs. After all, money was created to make your life easier, not more difficult. Ideally, what you do with your money should indicate your unique priorities in living and conducting business. This usually happens once you've come to terms with the value you attach to those little green and white pieces of paper.

Money, one of the most potent symbols in our culture, can be a measure of success, power, and self-worth. Our wealth can determine where we live, whom we associate with, and the person we marry. As Daniel Yankelovich points out in his book *New Rules*: "Money has many shared meanings, both practical and symbolic. Like sex in relation to love, the issue of money in relation to personal success is loaded with ambiguity."[2]

Let's take a moment to explore the multiple meanings of money. Here is an eclectic sampling of thoughts and sayings pertaining to money. (We've left some space for you to fill in some of your own cryptic remarks on the subject.)

$ "No one has ever been able to define what money is: A convenient medium of exchange so people do not have to haul their possessions around to barter? The fruits of past labor stored like grain in a silo for the future? The root of all evil? The conspiracy of governments?" (William G. Shepard, Jr., *New York Times*)

$ "Money makes money and that money makes more money." (Ben Franklin)

$ "I'm going to keep working. I've got to get away from all this money." (a forty-four-year-old New Jersey watchman, after winning a $5 million lottery)

$ "Worrying about money has nothing to do with how much money you have." (Jerry Gillies in *Moneylove*)

$ "I've been rich and I've been poor, and honey, there ain't no comparison." (Pearl Bailey)

$ "It's just as easy to live well when you're rich as when you're poor, but when you're poor it's much cheaper." (Andrew Tobias in *Getting By on $100,000 a Year*)

$ "I'm sexually satisfied, financially dissatisfied, and philosophically trying." (Mick Jagger)

$ "I don't care about making a lot of money; I just want to do my thing and get by." (typical attitude of many freelance artists in the sixties)

$ "I just want to do my thing and get by, but these days you need to be rich just to get by." (the above reinterpreted for the eighties)

$ "It's not the money, it's the *money*." (ace negotiator Herb Cohen, meaning: it's not the dollars per se, but their usefulness in keeping score)

$ "Money can't buy me love." (The Beatles)

$ (Your remarks here)

$

$

$

Now that we've looked at some general notions about money, sit down for a few minutes and get in touch with your own attitudes and feelings on the subject by answering the following questions:

HOW DO YOU FEEL ABOUT MONEY?

1. What does money represent in your life? (List in order of importance.)

    a.   Power   ....

    b.   Material possessions   ....

    c.   Freedom for leisure and travel   ....

    d.   Higher social standing   ....

    e.   More flexibility in how you work   ....

    f.   A feeling of greater security   ....

    g.   Other (explain)   ....

2. **What would a sudden windfall of money mean for you?**

    a. Ability to sustain your present lifestyle indefinitely with no financial strain   . . . .

    b. A complete revision in lifestyle   . . . .

    c. Different friends and new social contacts   . . . .

    d. More time to spend with your family   . . . .

    e. More time to do the kind(s) of work you really want to do   . . . .

    f. Other (explain)   . . . .

3. **How would you describe the way you deal with your finances?**

    a. I take care of my finances regularly.   . . . .

    b. I pay sporadic attention to my finances.   . . . .

    c. No problem—I like it.   . . . .

    d. I never look at them if I don't have to.   . . . .

    e. Why should I bother with finances? I always get by   . . . .

    f. Other.   . . . .

4. If you have an aversion to dealing with finances, which answer best describes why?

    a. My parents never dealt well with money and I acquired their attitudes. . . . .

    b. I'm afraid of what I'll find if I look. . . . .

    c. I'll mess up for sure. . . . .

    d. I don't know how to handle finances. . . . .

    e. I don't really know why I have an aversion to dealing with finances . . . I just do. . . . .

5. What would you do if you consistently fell short of your income objectives?

    a. Look for ways to work more effectively . . . .

    b. Change careers . . . .

    c. Take on more work . . . .

    d. Look for other kinds of freelance work . . . .

    e. Consider taking a nine-to-five job . . . .

    f. Alter lifestyle expectations . . . .

    g. Other (explain) . . . .

Don't be too concerned if you had problems answering some of these questions. It takes awhile to sort out one's feelings about money, and the issue has a lot of different sides. Nevertheless, many freelancers cling to the notion that their only financial concern is to generate as much money as possible. While this certainly is an important goal, it's only a beginning.

An increase in wealth does not necessarily correlate with a decrease in your financial—not to mention personal—problems. As Jack and Lois Johnstad observe in *The Power of Prosperous Thinking*: "Simply having more money [most often results] in raising the dollar level of (one's) financial problems. [Most people] would still suffer the same kinds of shortages and pinches, but in more expensive forms."[3] The Johnstads go on to say that no amount of money will provide financial peace of mind unless "there is an accompanying change in attitude and behavior—not only toward . . . money, but also toward wealth in general."

When you're struggling to pay the rent, it's hard to swallow the notion that a sudden windfall of money might create more problems than it solves. But unless you get a handle on your money and avoid escalating your expenses beyond your growing income, you are likely to become one of those people who look back on the good old carefree days when they were struggling just to get by. So instead of waiting for that distant coup that will take care of all your worries, learn to make the most of what you've got right now. Prepare yourself for the ups (hopefully) and downs (inevitably) that are part and parcel of working for yourself. Otherwise, dealing with money is always going to be a pain in the ass. Even when you've got lots of it.

A Crash Course in What Not to Do

Some of the most knowledgeable freelancers today became experts in what not to do by clearing up the financial disasters they created for themselves. Though we understand quite well that experience is the greatest teacher, we don't believe it's necessary to learn by making every mistake yourself. We'd like to think that if we had a book like this at the beginning of our careers, we could have avoided a lot of pain. One way to avoid costly mistakes is to learn from the experiences of others. With this in mind, we turn our attentions to the plight of Ron, a talented young musician who avoided so few pitfalls he's become a virtual object lesson in what not to do.

For the past year and half, Ron had been one of the busiest piano players in New York—with more offers for recordings and live gigs than he could handle. Just a few short months after graduating from college, he was earning over $800 a week. Not surprisingly, Ron started living high on the hog: He rented a lavishly furnished apartment in an expensive high-rise building. He bought himself a top-of-the-line sports car. One day, he received a letter in the mail that said the following: "You are among a select few people who have been chosen to receive a free Visa card. You have already been approved for a $1,000 line of credit."

Needless to say, Ron was thrilled. What a joy not to have to handle cash and to present this neat little piece of plastic at shops and restaurants all over town. Within a few months, Ron had been preapproved for several more credit cards. And the best part was, no matter how much money he ran up, the banks only asked for a small monthly payment. Ron quickly developed a taste for expensive clothes and fancy supper clubs. He especially enjoyed taking four or five people out for dinner, drinks, and a show and running up a $300 tab. When the check came, he just handed the waiter that magical plastic card to cover the whole deal.

Things were going smoothly for Ron, although it was now summer and he wasn't working as much as he had been the rest of the year. No problem. Ron wasn't about to compromise his lifestyle. He just made greater use of his credit cards and continued to buy whatever he wanted. Also, several banks offered Ron privileged checking. Not realizing that this was just another interest-bearing credit line for overdrawn checks, naturally Ron accepted this fountain of cash without hesitation. (After all, who was he to turn down such a privilege?)

Ron can't recall the exact day, but gradually it began to dawn on him that he was in serious financial trouble. First of all, he was overdrawn on all of his credit and privilege checking accounts. Nobody had explained that unless the full bill was paid every month, Ron was actually borrowing money from the banks at 19½ percent. Also, since a good deal of his income was received gross (i.e., before taxes) Ron owed the government thousands of dollars. Every day his mailbox was full of bills and terse letters from his creditors. His phone was ringing off the hook with calls from collection agencies asking him when he would pay up. Eventually, Ron stopped answering his phone, and soon, even his best friends and clients could no longer get in touch with him.

A few months later, Ron called to say that he had left New York and was currently living with his folks in the Midwest. He was working at local clubs and mailing his creditors small sums of money from the next county so that his address could not be traced. Ron hoped that these token payments would keep the wolf at bay for at least a little while. His creditors might not be thrilled, he reasoned, but at least they couldn't call him up or send him any more nasty letters.

Isn't it ironic that someone who spent so many years mastering the piano never even took one hour to acquire the most basic financial skills. If he had approached his music with a similar attitude, Ron probably would have never gotten past his second lesson. Then again, when you learn the piano, you have a teacher and method books explaining the various techniques. Nobody ever sat down with Ron and taught him the basics of handling money. Like so many of us, Ron grew up believing that the world of money was some faraway planet well beyond his grasp. Terms like interest rates, financial planning, and record-keeping sounded like so much mumbo jumbo. The only financial concept that ever crossed his mind was that if he could generate enough bucks, everything else would fall into place.

"I really screwed up my career and my personal life," Ron confided during a recent long-distance phone conversation. "I guess I jumped in blind and did all the wrong things." Ron made so many major mistakes, he had become a particularly valuable object lesson in what not to do.

It's Never Too Late (or Too Soon)

In spite of the mess he created for himself, there is a workable plan for Ron to reconstruct his financial situation, just as there is a workable plan for anyone who really wants to get a handle on their money. In most instances, the solutions are based on common sense rather than any intricate or technical financial knowledge.

What would you do if you were in Ron's shoes? Surely, there has to be a better answer than abandoning one's career and hiding out in another state. Imagine, for a moment, that you are one of Ron's creditors. What could he do to placate you short of completely clearing up his entire debt? If you're like most people, the single most important step might be a simple communication of good faith and intent to make things right. Business manager David Feinstein has dealt with many clients in the same boat as Ron. Here's what he tells them:

"Call up all of your creditors and tell them you have a lot of very heavy financial problems right now but you are trying your best to straighten them out. The worst thing you can do is to avoid the people that you owe money to. On the other hand, if you call them up and assure them that you intend to pay back every penny of what you owe, they will usually be willing to work

something out with you. They may not be crazy about the payment schedule you propose; but at that point, the pressure is on them to accept anything that's reasonable."

We will have more to say on how best to work the payment of existing debts into your financial plan. The important point is that no matter how little attention you've given these matters in the past or how much trouble you've gotten yourself into, there are effective and relatively simple steps you can take to get control of your financial situation. If you're just starting out or have been getting by without any major financial difficulties, you're in even better shape. By getting control of your money now, you are taking preventive measures that can lead to a more successful career and a happier personal life.

Avoid the Money Rut!!

W e've just seen what can happen to someone generating a sizable income if he takes no control over it. But an even more common problem among those who tune out their finances is an endless cycle that we call *The Money Rut*. People who get caught up in this cycle never seem to have enough money to do the things they want, experience feelings of desperation that cause them to take work they may dislike, and wind up spending most of their time involved in activities unrelated to their long-range lifestyle and career goals. Has anything like this ever happened to you?

THE MONEY RUT

1. You ignore your finances.

2. You find yourself caught short for money.

3. You accept work you should turn down just to alleviate your immediate bills and overwhelming feelings of anxiety and panic.

4. This leaves little or no time for career and lifestyle priorities.

5. You feel frustrated, unfulfilled, and helpless about your situation.

6. Cycle starts again.

We have developed a process that can get you out of your money rut—whatever form it may take—and put you at the helm of your financial ship. It is a highly flexible process, one that works for people at any stage of their career—and no matter

> You and your money: FROM MYSTERY TO MASTERY
>
> Mystery—your finances control you
>
> > Taking Stock
> >
> > > Awareness of unawareness
> > > Taking a look at where you've been
>
> Making the Most of What You've Got
>
> > > Finding opportunities for improvement
> > > Evaluating your situation
>
> Selecting the Best Alternatives
>
> > > Taking a positive approach to making choices
> > > Getting the information you need
> > > Establishing your priorities
> > > Developing good financial habits
>
> Mastery—you control your finances

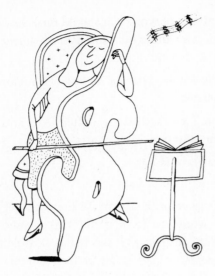

Achieving money mastery

how far gone their financial situation might seem. Because freelancers often design lifestyles based on their own unique values and priorities, we have designed a program that allows the individual to identify viable alternatives and decide how they fit into the total picture. Here then is a summary of this process that can take you from money mystery to mastery.

THE THREE-PHASE BUDGET

Phase 1: Taking Stock

As we see it, taking stock of your current financial situation is like getting on a scale. Recently, Joan launched a highly successful diet after months of procrastination. "What motivated you finally to get it going?" we asked. Joan's answer made a lot of sense:

"I knew I had put on a lot of weight." But I refused to get on a scale to see just how much. I tried to convince myself that I wasn't doing too badly, all the time knowing that the moment I got on that scale and saw the bad news in black and white, I'd have to do something about it. Once I saw how bad the problem had gotten, I immediately went on a diet. Now, I weigh myself every day. Instead of playing a lot of head games with myself, I let the scale give me the good or bad news."

The simple act of writing down your income (how much money comes in) and your expenses (how much money goes out) is an essential first step in clearing up your financial picture. Looking at your situation on paper helps you gain distance and self-control in handling your money. When things are written down, you can put them aside for a day and approach the information when you can best deal with it most effectively. If you like, you can even think of the numbers you write down as someone else's information that you are going to analyze. If, on the other hand, you refuse to put things in writing, everything about your finances—both real and imagined—remains in your head and you become like a person having both sides of an argument. You can't win. Once you get your finances out of your head and on paper, your thinking can begin to shift from a vague *somehow I'll manage* to a firm *this is how I want to manage*.

Let's, for a moment, pursue the analogy of dieting and budgeting a little further. If you were a hundred pounds overweight, you would go on a different kind of diet than if you were five pounds overweight. By the same token, you might take one plan of action if you were barely meeting your expenses every month, and another if your spending habits were putting you into heavy debt. In the latter case, you might decide to put yourself on a rather strict budget. Whatever your spending habits may be, you are always on some kind of a budget in the broadest sense. The money you make versus the money you spend constitutes your current budget, just as the food you eat versus the calories you burn up constitutes your current diet.

What all this means is that you are already on a budget even if you've never consciously established one. The fact is you do have some money coming in and some going out. The only thing you need to know in this first phase is how much money comes in and how much money goes out. Don't be too concerned that you might not like what you see once you've got the numbers written down. Many freelancers find that they are actually doing better than they imagined. Also, no matter what the numbers reveal, they are only a reflection of where you've been, not necessarily where you're heading.

✔ CHECKLIST ✔

Expenses

1. Monthly out of pocket expenses includes: carfare, food, entertainment, office supplies. List your own.
2. Fixed expenses (expenses which must be paid periodically) includes rent, utilities, insurance, mortgage taxes, loans, and credit card payments. List your fixed expenses.

Useful tips

1. Include all categories of expenses that pertain to you.
2. For phone, gas and electric, heating bills, look at a few typical months from past bills and estimate. For heating bills

be sure to include some winter and summer bills in your perusal.

3. If you are just starting to keep records of your monthly expenses, estimate for now and compare when you have the information documented.

Income

1. Fees
2. Royalties (includes residual payments)
3. Interest
4. Dividends
5. Other (personal sources of income not mentioned)

A good way to handle the record of your income is by using a ledger. This is just another name for a book used to keep track of money. A ledger can have different numbers of columns. For our purposes we need columns for the date, the amount, who it's from, and for what. A typical page may look like the one shown on page 74.

This is useful for record-keeping because it tells you how much you earned, for what work, and when it was paid. There are two ways to use a ledger.

1. Some people list the work they do in the ledger when it is performed. Then they enter the payment when it arrives and the date of payment.

2. Some people list the payments only when they arrive. They use a second notebook for accounts receivable (another name for money owed you for work done; see page 75).

We prefer the second way as it tells you in any given month what you earned. Also you have a separate source for what's owed you.

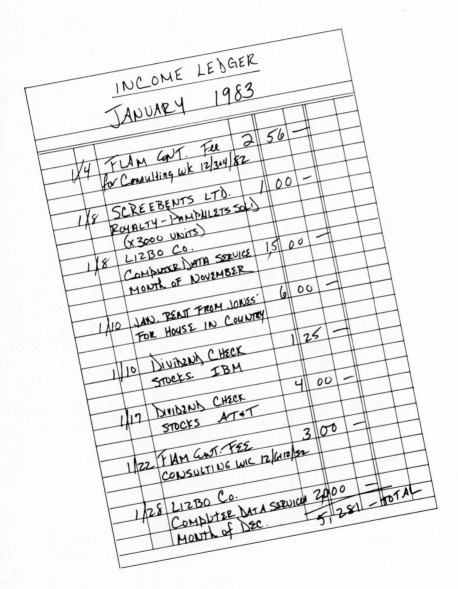

INCOME LEDGER
JANUARY 1983

1/4	FLAM CONT. FEE for Consulting wk 12/3+4/82	2	56 —
1/8	SCREEBENTS LTD. ROYALTY - PAMPHLETS SOLD (x 3000 UNITS)	1	00 —
1/8	LIZBO CO. COMPUTER DATA SERVICE MONTH OF NOVEMBER	15	00 —
1/10	JAN. RENT FROM JONES' FOR HOUSE IN COUNTRY	6	00 —
1/10	DIVIDEND CHECK STOCKS. IBM	1	25 —
1/17	DIVIDEND CHECK STOCKS AT+T	4	00 —
1/22	FLAM CONT. FEE CONSULTING WK 12/6+12/82	3	00 —
1/28	LIZBO CO. COMPUTER DATA SERVICE MONTH OF DEC.	2,000 —	5,281 — TOTAL

DATE	ACCTS. RECEIVABLE WHO - CLIENT + TERMS	JOHN WILSON - CONSULTANT AMT. DUE	DATE PD.
3/2	MEMO CORP. 6 HRS @ #35 hr. due 2wks 9AM-3PM	#210.00	✓ 3/26
3/7-10	MEMO CORP. 3 DAYS @ #270 DAY 9-5 due 2wks.	#810.00	✓ 4/8
3/12	XEBO BROS. min. 2hr. Consult to appraise their consulting needs #75 10-12 NOON due 30 days	#75.00	Call them!
3/14+15	XEBO BROS. 2days @ #270 day 9-5 due 30 days	#540.00	
3/18 3/19	DUNBAR Assoc. 4hrs @ #35 hr. " " " " " due 30 days	#140.00 #140.00	✓ 4/20 ✓ 4/20
3/23	MEMO CORP. 6 hr @ #35. hr. due 2wks	#210.00	✓ 4/26
3/27-28	Reynolds Assoc. 2days @ #270 day due 2wks	#540.00	✓ 4/28
3/30	Reynolds Assoc. 6 hrs @ #35. hr. FINISH PROJECT	#210	✓ 5/1

Useful tips

If you are just beginning to record your income, try to estimate it based on the knowledge you do have. If you have any past records use these as a basis for estimating.

Taking stock is the first important step in clearing up the financial mystery and gaining financial mastery. Once you've made it this far, the chances are good that you'll keep moving ahead.

Phase 2:
Making the Most
of What You've Got

A knowledge of your income and expenses will help you draw conclusions about how you conduct your business and personal finances. Which of these statements best describes you?

☐ I'm not earning enough money to cover my monthly expenses.

☐ I'm earning more than enough to cover my expenses, but I'm squandering it on things I can't identify.

☐ I'm covering my present expenses, but just barely.

☐ I need a lot more money to support my future lifestyle objectives.

☐ I'm making enough to support a comfortable lifestyle, but there are some expenses that I can cut down on.

☐ I'm content with my present financial situation. I see no need to either cut expenses or generate more income.

Most experts agree that the greatest opportunities for improving your budget are in adjusting your expenses. Discretionary expenses—like eating out and entertainment—can often be cut drastically, but even fixed expenses aren't cast in stone.

There are for example a number of effective ways to reduce your utilities bills. Mark, an engineering consultant, felt that his telephone bills were too high. Since he lives in Boston and transacts a lot of his business with clients on the West coast, he didn't see how he could substantially reduce his expense. However, he began taking advantage of the phone company's reduced rates during evening hours and discovered he could save between $55 and $75 every month. Other freelancers reduce expenses by finding ways to get needed services at a lower cost. Janet, a freelance copywriter, had been spending $80 a month for a personalized answering service. She recently bought an answering machine with a remote feature for picking up messages when she was out of her home-office for about $200. Her savings in the first year alone will amount to $760.

If you take a careful look at your expenses, you will probably find many relatively painless ways of cutting down. If your present budget shows that you are spending more than you make, you'll probably want to use any money you save via reduced expenses to get even. But what should a freelancer who is somewhat ahead of the game do with the additional monies generated by cutting expenses? Janet took the extra money she used to spend on her service and put it in a special vacations fund. Mark elected to put the money he saved on his phone bill into a retirement fund. If you find a way to cut down on an expense, don't just squander the money or put it in your checking account. Find a place to put it or a way to use it that has some impact on your life. Give yourself an incentive for cutting expenses by using the money you save for something positive in either your business or personal life.

As you analyze your budget, you'll find many opportunities for improvement. There are any number of creative solutions for an ailing budget: You can try to cut your expenses or find ways to raise your income. Bernard Meltzer illustrates how two general managers of a radio station approached this issue:

"We used to have a general manager who kept bringing up the [profits] of this station because his attitude was to spend a lot of money, but to bring in more than you spend. Now we have the reverse situation where the manager feels the best way is to save more than you spend. . . . Personally, I like the first way better."

In general, we feel that it is wise to cut expenses where feasible. On the other hand, we realize that some freelancers' greatest need is to generate more dollars. Should you decide that your energies could best be put to increasing your income, here are a few suggestions:

► Take on additional work in your field (subcontract that which you can't handle).

► Raise your prices.

► Seek work in a related field that is more lucrative.

► Take on some unrelated work on a part-time basis.

As you look over your budget and discover new and better ways to improve the relationship of what goes in to what goes out, keep in mind that the changes you make can have a positive impact on your business and personal life. The kinds of decisions you make in handling what you've got are nothing less than signposts of what your future will look like. As George Clason reminds us in *The Richest Man in Babylon*, the ultimate purpose of a budget is to attain not only necessities, but to "realize [your] most cherished desires by defending them from [your] casual wishes."[4]

Phase 3:
Selecting the Best Alternatives

Let's get back for a moment to the most basic need for a budget. If only you could win that million-dollar lottery or inherit that fortune from that proverbial long-lost relative, you could—in theory—spend as much as you please on whatever you please. Luckily for most of us, there are less random—albeit slower—ways to become wealthy. The majority of rich people reach that lofty plateau not through some sudden windfall, but through a series of well-considered choices. As economist Leonard Silk points out in *Economics in Plain English*: "Since resources are finite and scarce, you can ordinarily satisfy one want by not satisfying another want."[5] This concept is known as *opportunity cost*, or what you give up to do one thing by not doing something else.

Say you've cut down on a few expenses and have an extra $100 available to you each month. What should you do with it? After all, money itself has no value beyond what you do with it:

You can't eat it; you can't make love to it; you can't wear it. Here are some things that you can do with your money:

$ Buy goods and services you want and need now

$ Improve your present lifestyle

$ Improve your business

$ Invest to earn more money

$ Provide a cushion for the future

$ Protect against expenses due to illness and unforeseen disasters

$ Allow greater freedom in your work

$ Increase leisure activities

$ Spend on impulse because it makes you feel good

Keeping the concept of opportunity cost in mind, get comfortable with the notion that if you spend your money on A, you're not going to have as much to spend on B. But this is not deprivation in any sense of the word. It is, rather, the selection of alternatives that have the greatest or most immediate value to you. Say on a given Saturday night you were deciding to go to either a movie or a play and finally chose the play. You wouldn't expend any energy fretting over the terrific flick you were missing. Unless you're extremely masochistic, you'd try your best to enjoy the entertainment at hand. If you've been putting off creating a budget for yourself because you're afraid you'll have to give things up, try taking this positive approach to your choices. In other words, enjoy and utilize what you've got.

There are no absolutes on how to structure your budget. It's your money; nobody but you can decide the best ways to use it. Once you understand the alternatives and identify the ones that matter to you most, those are the things you work into your budget first.

We've spoken to a number of experts familiar with the kinds of finances situations that people who work for themselves are likely to run into. Even though there often is a remarkable consensus on what these experts suggest, nothing is written in stone. The pages that follow provide basic information you will need to make those decisions that reflect your unique priorities.

TAXES AND RECORD-KEEPING

BEFORE WE DISCUSS OTHER FINANCIAL MATTERS IT behooves us to look at taxes—an event, the cliché tells us, about as inevitable as death itself. Alas, we must all pay taxes whether we are salaried employees, self-employed, or a combination of both. The picture is somewhat brighter, however, if at least part of your income is earned through self-employment. There are any number of tax deductions the IRS allows self-employed persons to deduct. Here is a partial listing:

Rent for your place of business
Phone and utilities that apply to your work
Business-related travel expenses
Tuition fees for courses that relate to your work
Transportation to and books for these courses

Entertainment—business related

Gifts to clients

Taxis to and from business appointments

Trade publications

Video and audio equipment—if required for your business

Repairs on equipment

Purchases of equipment and supplies

Postage

Photocopying expenses

Answering machine or service

IRA and Keogh contributions

Legal services

Automobile for business purposes

Business cards and stationery

Accounting and financial services

Credit card interest—business related

Dues for unions and professional organizations

Advertising and public relations expenses

Moving costs

Meals with clients and potential clients

Your accountant will advise you exactly which deductions apply to your business. One thing that he (or she) is sure to tell you is that the responsibility for proving all expenses falls squarely on your shoulders, and that means keeping records. If you are the type who simply refuses to maintain records, you might either be losing a bundle on deductions to which you are entitled, or taking deductions without documentation and leaving yourself open for problems with the IRS.

"People who work for themselves need to keep better records than employees, because the burden of record production is on their shoulders," says Bill Bresnan. "The IRS wants to know where your hours are spent, what your hours have produced, and what your hours have cost. The best way to document these things is by notations in a diary or datebook."

Proper documentation of an expense means writing down who you were with, where you were, and what you were doing for what business purpose. The notation can be made on the back of a receipt as well as in a diary. "If an expense exceeds $25," David Feinstein points out, "you must have a receipt. For maximum safety, I recommend both entering the expense in a diary *and* keeping the receipt."

Since you can't very well call up your accountant every time you want to make certain a particular expense can be applied to your business, the best thing to do is to save all receipts that might be at all relevant to your work. As discussed in Chapter One, there are a number of ways to get much of your record-keeping work done for you. Here is a partial listing:

☆ Use one credit card only for business. Your monthly statement is acceptable as documentation.

☆ Keep a separate checking account for all business-related expenditures.

☆ Set up accounts with regular suppliers, pay them by check and keep the monthly bills.

Taxes are complex and best left in the hands of your accountant. Aside from the record-keeping aspect, however, there are a few crucial areas that all freelancers should be aware of, namely:

Planning ahead for your tax expense

Because most self-employed persons do not have taxes withheld from their earnings, it is essential that you have some idea of what your tax bite will be and put some money aside. One of the biggest problems that freelancers encounter is that they spend the money that they owe the government, and leave themselves short at tax time. Your accountant should be able to give you an estimate of how much your taxes are likely to be in a given year. If he or she tells you that you are going to have to give approximately 25 percent to the government, you would be wise to take that money off the top of every check you receive and put it in a high-interest, liquid account. But remember: *That money isn't savings, it is an anticipated expense.*

Getting audited

The IRS has a more difficult time keeping track of freelancers than of salaried employees. Therefore, some people reason, they are more likely to audit you if all or part of your income comes from self-employment. In fact, nobody is certain who will be audited and when. We do know that a certain percentage of returns are selected at random for auditing (some sources put this figure at one-half of one percent). It has also been established that your chances of being audited are greater if you earn over $50,000 a year. (This makes sense since, given their limited manpower, the IRS would rather go after bigger fish.) In any case, an audit is nothing to get unduly upset about *if* you can produce proper documentation to back up your expenses.

There are a number of gray areas in self-employment deductions. One of the most difficult areas involves the deduction of part of your apartment as a home-office. Technically, the space you use for your work is supposed to be exclusively for that purpose. But, in fact, many freelancers in large urban areas live and work out of a one-room studio. Not wanting to trigger an audit, some accountants have discouraged such freelance clients from taking the home-office deduction, even though their apartments actually were their sole base of operations. Recently, the IRS has allowed such deductions if it can be shown that the space used for work—even if not a separate room—is used exclusively for that purpose.

Your accountant will tell you which deductions to claim on your taxes; his or her reticence or aggressiveness in this area should not be at odds with your own tendencies. You don't want someone so sleazy that your return screams out to be audited. On the other hand, you want to be sure that your accountant takes every single deduction to which you are legally entitled. No less an authority than former IRS commissioner Russell C. Harrington has counseled: "Every tax payer has a right to adjust his affairs so that he minimizes his tax liability. . . . Tax evasion is illegal. Tax avoidance isn't."

Even if you've been overly conservative in claiming your deductions, there is still a chance that you will be audited. What to do? "If your income is less than $30,000 a year and your records are in order, you'll walk right through the audit," says David Feinstein, who feels that people in this category don't need to bring their accountant with them. For those earning upwards of $50,000 a year, Feinstein urges that their accountant be present at the audit. Although many people have gone through audits with no problems, some get so nervous that it is worth the expense of having their accountant present. In any event, you should ascertain your accountant's charges and feelings about accompanying you to an audit, should it become necessary. The following guidelines may be helpful if the IRS calls you in.

HOW TO HANDLE AN AUDIT

If you are given the option of where to schedule the audit, have it conducted in your accountant's office or the IRS office. This is particularly crucial if you use part of your home as an office.

Bring only those records that relate to the area being looked into. Don't bring up any other areas of your business that you are not asked about.

If possible, don't postpone the meeting. Arrive on time and dress conservatively.

Make sure all relevant records are neatly organized. If you hand the agent a lot of crumpled-up receipts, the agent is not going to look upon you with much delight.

If your accountant is with you, let him or her do most of the talking. If you are asked to speak, answer specific questions briefly; do not attempt to make small talk with the agent.

If your records are in order, you have nothing to be especially nervous about. Even if a deduction is disallowed, you'll only be asked to pay that amount plus interest.

If you do not like the result of your audit, you can and should appeal the decision in tax court. If the amount in question is under $5,000, you do not need a lawyer and can argue your case yourself.

Some Additional Benefits of Good Record-Keeping

One of the keys to maximizing your tax situation is establishing and maintaining good record-keeping systems. As we've said, any accountant will tell you that this is the first rule of avoiding problems with the IRS. Since you have to keep records, there is no reason to ignore the valuable information they give you about your business. If you learn to use and interpret your records correctly, they become a kind of free consultant that can help you streamline your operation and point you in the right direction. Here are some vital kinds of information you can glean from your records:

What Your Records Tell You

☆ which work pays you best

☆ which projects are a waste of time

☆ where to best focus your energies

SURROUND YOURSELF WITH EXPERTS

ON A TV TALK SHOW, SONGWRITER-ACTOR KRIS Kristofferson stated that the best thing about making a lot of money is that he can now afford to hire someone to take care of all his finances without ever having to think of these matters himself. This attitude is not uncommon among freelancers.

"Many self-employed people don't have the inclination, ability, and desire to get involved in handling their money," says David Feinstein. "When they do get involved with things like basic bookkeeping, bill paying, and financial planning, they find them tedious and handle them in a half-ass way."

For a tax deductible 5 percent a year, Feinstein recommends that anyone making over $50,000 a year hire themselves a competent, trustworthy business manager who will do everything from filling out expense diaries to finding the most advantageous tax-sheltered investments. All well and good. But does this mean that freelancers in higher financial brackets can just put all their money matters in someone else's hands?

"Your business advisors are your servants," says Bernard Meltzer. "You should listen to what they say but make the decisions yourself." Singer Dolly Parton—recognized as one of the smartest women in show business—has a similar approach in employing experts. "I own me," she declares. "I will pay [lawyers and accountants] for advice, but I will make the final decisions myself."[6]

If you're like most people, you probably haven't got the time or inclination to spend the better part of your energies looking after your money. Whether you make $5,000 or $5 million a year, you are going to need some assistance handling this aspect of your career. But no matter how far along you are in your financial picture and how much power you delegate, you are ultimately responsible for what happens to your money. Even business managers like David Feinstein who often find that "freelancers need someone to help them, to mother them along by making things orderly and clear," makes it a point to tell all of his clients: "You should be responsible for knowing what is going on. If you don't understand 100 percent of what I'm doing, you're not using me properly." It takes time and experience to understand the ins and outs of handling your money. Picking the right people to help you, however, is a far less complicated process.

Accountants

The first financial expert you should select is a competent accountant who is familiar with your field. If you are earning enough money to file a tax form, you're almost certain to come out ahead if you let an accountant fill it out. Any decent accountant is almost certain to save you more money than his tax deductible fee. Also, your accountant can be an important business contact and a big help in selecting other financial specialists.

When you pick an accountant, find out what services are provided outside of preparing your taxes. "A reputable accountant isn't just there to grind out tax returns," says Bill Bresnan. "Anyone who just fills out forms in exchange for a fee is nothing more than a hack: You can get anyone to do that. Good accountants who care about maintaining their professional reputations will get involved on some kind of regular basis."

When you interview prospective accountants, ask if their basic tax-time bill includes consultations during the course of the year. It isn't reasonable to expect a lot of free advice, but you shouldn't be billed every time you have a five-minute phone conversation. As with any professional you work with, you want someone reputable enough to be an asset to your business, but who is not so busy that you end up being treated like a tiny fish in an enormous lake. This doesn't mean that you should shy away from top professionals. Even the best accountants and other financial experts will sometimes take on a client in the early stages of their career if they get a good feeling about that person's potential.

One important issue that you want to be sure to broach with your accountant is whether his or her fee includes accompanying you to a tax audit should you be called down for one. Many accountants do not build this cost into their fees, opting to charge only as the need arises. In any case, you want to know that your accountant will accompany you if needed and what the charge will be.

In selecting accountants and other members of your financial team, you should use a commonsense approach. "The best way to find an accountant or other financial expert," counsels Carol O'Rourke, vice-president for marketing at Smith Barney in New York, "is similar to the way you find a doctor," namely:

- Ask friends or others in your field for referrals.

- Ask the person for two references of professionals in your field with whom he works, and contact those people. Don't work with anyone who refuses to give you references.

- Request an initial in-person meeting (there should be no charge for this).

- See at least two or three different people. Don't work with anyone who makes you feel uncomfortable.

In his book *How to Beat the Salary Trap*, Richard Rifenbark offers some useful guidelines of what he looks for in a professional, whether financial or otherwise:

> We are compatible; we talk on the same wavelength; our heads are in the same place. When I need the answer to a question, I get it accurate and well thought out. When he doesn't know the answer immediately, he doesn't double talk or do a soft shoe shuffle around it. "I'll get back to you," he says. And he does. He is generous with information so that I soon learn the right questions to ask. There is a spirit of "we" about our dealings whether "we" good or "we" bad. I feel that he is an interested participant in my business.[7]

Attorneys

Though not strictly a part of your day-to-day financial life, there are any number of matters that can require the services of an attorney, be they contract negotiations, copyright disputes, real estate closings, or wills. It would be prudent to get to know a lawyer before you actually need his or her services. You can do this by getting a few referrals, calling them up, and telling them that though you don't require their services right now, you will in the future. That way, you won't have to lay the basic groundwork when you are under pressure. Keep in mind that, like physicians, lawyers tend to specialize. For the most part, you wouldn't use the same lawyer to iron out a copyright dispute as you would to close a real estate deal. Legal specialists are often quite expensive, but the price of using someone who can't handle your required situation correctly is hardly a bargain.

Bankers

One financial expert who charges nothing for his services, but who can help you in a variety of situations is an officer of your bank with whom you have a good working relationship. In his book *The ABC's of IRA's*, William J. Grace, Jr. aptly sums up the need for a good banking relationship:

> If you don't already have a person whom you can identify as "your banker," then I would recommend [taking the] . . . opportunity to start a relationship that could help you in [a number of] financial matters. Your bank can help you with any of the following: getting a quick loan in an emergency situation . . . financing assistance and advice on a real estate transaction, advice on getting legal or tax assistance, help in planning overseas travel,

help in getting cash or credit if you are out of town, safe deposit boxes, help in estate settlements, retirement planning, and general financial planning. Your banker may also be a valuable business contact for you because of his or her familiarity with business and other professional people in your community.[8]

Insurance Agents

Most experts recommend that you get two agents—one for life insurance and one for coverage of your property. "Try to deal with agents who are independent and represent more than one company," Bill Bresnan advises. "They can shop around to find you the best deal."

Low rates are important, but they aren't the only consideration in selecting an insurance agent. Writes Bonnie Siverd in *Working Woman* magazine:

An insurance policy is nothing more than a piece of paper until you need it. But the quality of an agent's company and service is of paramount importance when you file a claim. Ask how long it takes to settle the average claim as well as a contested one. If an agent recommends a policy from a company you do not know, look it up in *Best's Insurance Reports* found in many libraries. Give priority to companies with an A or A-plus rating. The prices and products of lower ranked firms may not be competitive.[9]

When shopping around for insurance, keep in mind that the agent's commission may be greater on some policies than others.

Make sure you are getting the one that's best for you, not for him. Your accountant can be a useful consultant in selecting an insurance agent and the kinds of policies that are right for you.

Stockbrokers

If you are ready to invest in stocks and/or bonds (see page 107 for what to take care of before investing), there are any number of brokers ready and eager to handle your transactions. Before you get your feet wet, however, it pays to learn about the kinds of investment options that are available. You can call up any of the major brokerage houses and speak to the broker of the day, who will be happy to answer any questions and send you a variety of informative written material. In fact, we recommend that you call for these free materials—even if you have no immediate thought of investing—just as a source of useful information. If, on the other hand, you are serious about the market, use the same formula for selecting a broker that you did for your other advisors. As far as the impact that any particular broker is likely to have on your success, Andrew Tobias offers the following opinion:

> There *are* no brokers who can beat the market consistently and by enough of a margin to more than make up for their brokerage fees. Or if there are a few, they are not going to work for peanuts. Or if they will—because they are just starting out in the business or have a soft spot in their heart for you—*there's no way for you to know who they are.*[10]

Business Managers

If you are in such a high tax bracket that you have to shelter a good deal of your money, or if you are so turned off by financial matters that you absolutely need someone to handle it all for you, it might be a good move to get yourself a business manager who knows you and your business. Business managers are often accountants or attorneys who bring in other experts to handle specific areas of your finances. As noted before, the 5 percent fee they usually charge is tax deductible. If the manager is throwing in his or her accounting or legal services as part of the fee, the numbers look even better. Some experts don't think it is advisable to have your accountant be your business manager. In any case, if you think this kind of relationship would help you gain financial control, you should keep in mind that you are delegating a large portion of responsibility and power to someone else. Make sure that the person is competent, trustworthy, and otherwise suited to handle such an important aspect of your life.

David Feinstein explains the function of the business manager this way: "You should go out and generate the dollars, and have faith in your business manager to take care of the financial aspects of those dollars. The business manager should be able to save and invest money for the client, pay the client's bills, and, if necessary, do follow-up and collection work on a limited basis."

Financial Planners

For the most part, financial planners help you get an overview of your present needs and future strategies. Some people go to a financial planner first and let them help select other experts to work with. This can work out well if the advice you are getting from your planner is impartial. However, you want to make certain that he or she is not steering you in a direction that puts more money in his or her pockets than yours. If, for example, your financial planner is an insurance specialist, you want to be certain that there is no bias toward selling you products that bring the highest commissions. Like any other good advisor, a reputable financial planner should be more concerned with your long-term interests and his or her professional standing than the fast buck.

CREDIT

FOR YEARS, TV COMMERCIALS HAVE BEEN INVITING us to dine at the best restaurants, buy fashionable clothes at overpriced boutiques, travel to exotic islands, and so on. With one or two easy-to-get credit cards, you can also receive thousands of dollars with no questions asked and do anything you want with the money. Welcome to the wonderful world of credit and credit cards, your golden key to the good life. There's just one catch: Every cent has to be paid back. If the full amount isn't paid back within the specified time period (usually thirty days) you will be charged a healthy interest rate—currently $19\frac{1}{2}$ percent—on the unpaid balance.

We've seen how the abuse of credit can get you into serious trouble, so why not just determine to live within your means and pay cash for everything? For one thing, self-employed people often go through periods when cash is tight. Sometimes, you can wait for months to be paid for completed work. There are also slow months in most freelance businesses when very little cash is coming in. In fact, few independent contractors can anticipate a consistent amount of cash coming in, even if their annual income is substantial. That's why credit and credit cards can be useful if you learn how to handle them properly.

Let's say you've been thinking about buying a small computer for your business. Although you are going to have to shell out several thousand dollars to get the unit you need, you anticipate saving many hours getting your work done. The computer you want is on sale for $2,500.00 and your accountant thinks it would be a good investment from a tax standpoint. It's now the middle of November and you anticipate little or no cash coming in until January, at which time you expect to collect $6,500.00 for work already billed out. You've got some money in your savings account, but you've decided not to touch that. The solution is simple. You've got two bank credit cards—a Mastercard and Visa—with $1,500.00 credit lines, $3,000.00 in all. You decide to buy the computer by taking a cash advance on your credit cards, intending to pay in full within the billing period. Even if some of your clients are late in paying you and you can't pay the computer off until the following month, the interest would only be $37.50 ($2,500.00 × 1½% interest for one month), part of which you can deduct from your taxes. Since the computer is currently on sale for half of its usual $5,000.00 price, buying it now would be an intelligent, constructive use of your credit cards.

The other side of the credit coin are those people who become credit card junkies. These are the folks who the banks and other credit card companies have directed much of their advertising campaigns at. We are constantly being encouraged to over-consume and get into debt at 19½ percent a year. Avoid this at all costs.

"Credit was designed to buy buildings, machinery, and other real assets," says Bill Bresnan, "not to buy pantyhose. I feel that credit cards are a disease that plays with you psychologically. When you reach into your pocket for a fifty-dollar bill, you've got tremendous respect for that fifty bucks. But when you put down a piece of plastic to pay for something, you don't feel as if you're spending real money, so you've got no respect for it."

CREDIT CARD JUNKIE

"Don't leave home without me!"

To reap the benefits without suffering the disease of credit cards, you must know how to use them properly. Basically, this means paying all charges before interest accrues. If, on occasion, you decide to buy something and pay if off with interest, make sure the charges are included in your overall financial plan. Once you get a handle on your credit spending, you will find those little plastic cards useful in a number of ways. Here are a few:

You get a vital source of identification. If you've ever tried to rent a car without a credit card, you know just how valuable one can be. In certain instances, a credit card is the only piece of valid I.D. that will be accepted.

You get an accurate record-keeping system. If you use one card strictly for business, you get a receipt at the time of purchase plus a monthly itemized bill. This is an automatic form of record-keeping that can save you time when you do your taxes.

You get free use of money for twenty-five to fifty-five days. If you make purchases or take cash advances on the day after the billing date (indicated on the top of your monthly statement), you have fifty-five days to pay it off. Under any circumstances, you have at least thirty interest-free days before payment is due.

Getting and Keeping Credit

Credit cards are just the beginning of the credit story because they are the most visible and often the easiest type of credit to obtain. But if you are ever going to finance a major purchase—such as a home or a significant expansion of your business, you will probably have to take out a loan. This is often a difficult process for the self employed, because without proof of a steady income, the banks are hesitant to lend money. One of the truest clichés about credit is that banks only want to lend money to those who can prove they don't need it. That's why it is wise to:

Establish good credit before you need it

"Open up a passbook savings account," advises Bill Bresnan. "Then take out a passbook loan, pay it back early, and you'll be in credit heaven. Say you have $5,000 in your passbook savings account and take a loan for $2,000. You're getting the best rate of interest because your loan is secured by the money in the account. . . . Plus, you can write part of the interest expense off on your taxes."

Apply for credit cards and establish as much credit as soon as possible. If you have a regular job now and plan to be self-employed in the future, start building a positive credit picture today. If your spouse has credit cards and you have a problem obtaining them, try to get a second card on his or her name. After a few months, if you pay your bills on time, the banks will begin offering you credit cards in your own name.

Another wise preliminary step to take that can improve your chances of getting credit when you need it is to talk to an officer of your bank. Let him or her know about your business and plans for future growth. Because of the way freelancers' tax returns are structured, bankers often have problems assessing their suitability for credit. David Feinstein explains:

> "If self-employed people prepare their returns properly and take as many deductions as they possibly can, the chances are their gross income has been substantially reduced by all these expenses. If they earn $50,000 a year, their taxable income might be down to $18,000. The bank looks very skeptically at this and asks, 'How do you expect me to give you a loan when your taxable income is so low?' This also comes up when freelancers apply for credit cards."

Feinstein gets around this obstacle by writing a letter to the banker explaining the circumstances. If you can do enough to show the banker that you are a good credit risk, you will get the loan.

"Freelancers have a lot of positive aspects for credit," Bernard Meltzer points out, "because they are the masters of their own destiny, but they have to make out the application right. If they say their income fluctuates or that they make

$10,000 a year, they probably won't get a loan—even with a good credit history. I once got an open line of credit for $300,000 upon my signature, and the same day I got turned down for a credit card by the same bank because I made the application for the credit card out wrong. . . . I wrote that I was self-employed and that my income varied widely."

Don't screw up your credit

"If you were the bank evaluating your application for a loan," asks Bill Bresnan, "would you smile or would you throw up?" As difficult as it can be for self-employed people to establish credit, and as essential as it is for survival, it behooves you to do what you can to maintain a good credit standing. "Credit should be the first thing you take care of before any other bills," says David Feinstein. "Because once you screw up your credit, you're going to have a lot of trouble with it later on. A lot of clients come to me after they have already lost their credit and it often takes many years for me to get it back for them."

Some people with severe credit problems opt for declaring bankruptcy. This process, in effect, absolves them of all debts but often permanently hinders their ability to get credit in the future. Because of the importance of credit to self-employed people, most of our experts consider bankruptcy an unwise solution to settling debts. "Avoid declaring bankruptcy," counsels David Feinstein. "It's going to mess up your credit in the future, so stay away from it. I believe in people honoring their obligations as much as possible."

Taking care of back debts

If you agree that owning up to your responsibilities is the honorable way to go, you will want to work out a program to settle your debts. Even if your problems are such that you might be tempted to forgo your honor, remember you might need to raise money in the future, so you don't want to be known as a deadbeat.

As we saw earlier with our piano-playing friend Ron, your creditors really don't have much choice but to accept some kind of reasonable repayment plan from you. Most experts advise that you budget a certain percentage of your income each month for back debts. Some, like Erna Ferris, think that it sometimes helps to consolidate debts and take one loan to immediately settle all back debts and have only one creditor. "This method isn't necessarily cheaper," she points out. "But it can be psychologically easier."

"The worst thing you can do is avoid your creditors," says Bill Bresnan, reflecting the consensus of all our experts. "The best thing you can do is to face them—call or write each one and tell them exactly what the problem is. Once you spell it out for them, you'll invariably find that they will work something out with you. They want to get their money."

If you are dealing with banks, stores, and the like, it might be a good idea to let your accountant get involved. He or she can help you devise a budget and decide how much you can realistically afford to pay back each week or each month. Here's how David Feinstein helps resolve these matters for his clients:

> "When we establish the payment program, we allow for the payback before certain luxuries for the individual who owes the money. Then, I contact all the companies monies are owed to and tell them that I will be involved in trying to work out a payment program for them. Then I try to get as good terms as I possibly can. Sometimes I just tell them what we are going to do, and if they don't like it, too bad."

While it's true that as the debtor you've got a certain amount of power in the situation (after all, you've already spent their money), you may want to take a different approach when the creditors are friends or relatives who loaned you the money—usually with no interest—on the basis of trust. After all, these people stood by you when you needed help, and you want to maintain their goodwill—not to speak of your own sense of integrity—by honoring your commitments. The same principle of explaining your situation and working out some kind of reasonable payment program applies here as with banks and companies. We're all human and prone to mistakes. If your mistakes have been in the area of back debts, start a positive program that will put you on good footing not only with your creditors, but more importantly, with yourself.

SAVINGS

> I was sustained by the determination that this
> would be a slob summer for McGee. It wouldn't be a
> gaudy summer. There wasn't enough bread for that. But a
> careful husbanding of funds would see me
> through, leaving the emergency fund untapped, ready to
> finance some kind of operation in the fall. Freelance salvage
> consultant Travis McGee in John D. McDonald's
> *Bright Orange for the Shroud*[11]

If there is one certainty about working for yourself, it is financial uncertainty at every level—from struggling beginner to successful veteran. Since generally there is no regular weekly paycheck to count on, financial experts stress the need for freelancers to begin a regular savings program at the earliest stages of your career, and stick with it through thick and thin. Here are some useful guidelines for structuring such a program.

Setting Up a Basic Emergency Fund

No matter how much (or little) you are earning, you should immediately start building a cushion against slow earning periods or unforeseen events that reduce your income potential. Bill Bresnan advises self-employed persons to keep at least two months' total expenses in an interest-bearing account that you can get to in a hurry: "If you spend $2,500 a month, you should have $5,000 in a passbook or other liquid account as a basic emergency fund." Other experts feel that six months' expenses provides a more realistic degree of safety against the insecurities of freelancing. Ultimately, you will have to decide on how much of a cushion you require—based on the nature of your particular business and how well you sleep at night. But remember, the knowledge that you've got the funds to carry you through those lean periods can greatly reduce the time and energy you spend worrying about money.

As we discovered in Chapter One, it is almost always possible to generate some savings, even if you are living rather close to the line. As Rifenback so astutely advises in *How to Beat the Salary Trap*, "Better interrogate your expenses before you convict your income."[12] In other words: learn to live on less than what you earn. If you develop this habit while your income is low, you'll have confidence and cash for the future. The amount that you save is far less important than the commitment to save on a regular basis. Traditionally, 10 percent was used as a guideline for how much should be funneled into savings, though 5 percent might be a more realistic figure. The key is to make saving a consistent and automatic part of your life.

Once you are meeting your monthly bills, have a substantial cushion for emergencies, and have developed the habit of putting something away regularly, there is something you should keep in mind that people in their struggle to get by often forget.

You Deserve to Keep
Part of What You Earn

Unless you see yourself as someone who wants nothing more than to pay the bills, you should never forget that you are entitled to use some of your money for things you want, no matter how tight your budget sometimes gets. After all, the reason most of us are working is to improve the quality of our lives. So no matter how close you have to cut it some months, no matter how pressing certain expenses might seem, you are always entitled to keep some of the money you earn for yourself.

Create specific funds for the things you want

Have you been thinking about buying a home computer, taking a couple of weeks to lay on some exotic beach, refurbishing your wardrobe? You can save for these things by putting a few dollars each week into a specific account that you designate for a particular purpose. Don't put that money into your checking account; you'll soon lose track of it. Make sure you end up using the money for its intended goal by starting a vacation fund, home computer fund, clothing fund, etc. When you've accumulated a sufficient sum, take the money out and use it for its designated purpose.

If you think that your present income doesn't offer you enough leeway for specific savings funds, here's a system that can turn your loose change into significant sums of money almost without effort.

Dave's jar

While we were interviewing Dave, a cabinetmaker, we noticed an enormous amount of change that he had dumped from a huge jar onto his bed. As we spoke, he casually rolled the quarters, dimes, nickels, and pennies he had saved. "I've got over $300 here—four and a half months of putting all my change into the jar. This weekend, I'm renting a car and taking my girlfriend away for a few days." We asked him how long he'd been saving change in the jar. "I've been putting change in the jar for over three years now." Here's Dave's method:

$ Don't spend your change.

$ Create change. Always give a bill for small items.

$ At the end of each day, put all your change in the jar and don't touch it!!

$ If for any reason you absolutely must use some of the change, pay it back with a dollar bill.

Save Now for Future Wealth

"Wealth is accumulated," George Clason tells us in *The Richest Man in Babylon*, first in small sums, then in larger ones as a person learns and becomes more capable.[13] Once you've created your emergency cushion and successfully saved for a few specific desires, you might want to think a little bit more about your long-term financial growth. Perhaps you would like to own your own home some day, or raise a family, or make a significant investment in a new business. Even if you haven't given much thought to these things, you probably have thought about improving your financial picture in the future. Most financial experts tend to agree with Clason that a commitment to a regular, long-term savings program is the key to wealth. That's why we believe that you should put approximately half of your savings away for the future. The money can go toward retirement, buying a house, raising a family, or substantially expanding your business. Even if you are not altogether certain about how you want to use those funds, your long-term savings should be thought of as money that you contract with yourself not to touch for years to come.

Where to put what money

Because commitment and regularity are the most important elements of a successful savings program, it isn't terribly important that you spend a lot of time hassling with numerous bank accounts. Since most banks now offer high-interest accounts that are both safe (federally insured) and liquid (you can get to your

TABLE I

Emergency Cushion—In a separate, insured, high-interest, liquid account.

Dave's Jar—A simple, painless way to turn dimes and quarters into tangible goals.

Specific Funds—One or more separate accounts to take care of short-range goals.

Long-Term Savings—Often, you can obtain a higher interest rate by tying up your money for six months, one year or more. If you have enough of a cushion, this might be a good way of assuring that you won't dip into that money.

Retirement Accounts—Keoghs and IRAs (see page 107, Retirement).

money if you need it in a hurry), they are good places to keep your money. While any system of saving is valid if it works for you, we prefer one that lets you know which monies are going for what. Table I sums up the kind of multipurpose program we suggest.

As your wealth increases and your financial picture gets more complex, you may want to look into some kinds of investments, such as stocks, mutual funds, bonds, real estate, etc. Each of these investment options requires a book to itself, and you don't want to take any risks with your money without consulting your accountant and other members of your financial team. We would like to note, however, that most experts agree that you should not even think about taking any risks with your money until you have laid a strong financial foundation. Carol O'Rourke lists four categories that should be taken care of before you even explore any investment options. These are:

1. Enough income to cover your expenses

2. Enough insurance including: health, disability, fire and theft, and life (if necessary)

3. Adequate liquid reserves—money you can get to in a hurry at least enough to live on for two months

4. A tax-deferred retirement plan such as a Keogh and/ or IRA

Retirement:
Investing Now for Your Future

"There are very few truly good things in the world, but IRAs and Keoghs are two of them. In fact, anyone who qualifies to set up a Keogh Plan or IRA and doesn't is making a very big mistake," says Andrew Tobias.[14]

If you're still relatively young and have trouble socking away money for potential needs six months down the road, thoughts of saving for retirement probably seem about as remote as going to the moon. Yet virtually every financial expert we've come across echoes Carol O'Rourke's feelings on the subject:

"The very first thing I advise freelancers to do is to think about their retirement, no matter what their age. . . . The self-employed have a big advantage over people who work nine-to-five jobs in that they can open a Keogh account.

"A Keogh is a way that the government has finally helped freelancers. Any self-employed person—including doctors—can put up to $30,000 a year into any kind of investment. Let's say you have a good year and make $120,000; you can put up to 15 percent of your taxable income, or $18,000, in Keogh (as of September 1, 1984)."

If you're still not convinced that retirement should be a consideration at this point in your life, consider these two facts:

☐ The money you put into Keoghs and IRAs are tax deductible in the year they are invested.

☐ The interest these accounts earn cannot be taxed until you start taking the money out—between ages fifty-nine and one-half and seventy.

Let's pretend for a moment that you are a consultant in your twenties earning $25,000 a year. You never seem to have much money left over for savings, and retirement planning has never entered your mind. When you sit down with your accountant at tax time, he tells you that if you don't put $1,200 into a Keogh, you'll pay a good deal of it in taxes. It dawns on you that though your golden years are a good way off, the money you pay in taxes to the government is out of your hands forever, and that's even more remote than retirement.

In effect, the government is offering you the following choice: *Invest the money for your future or hand over the taxes on it to us now.* Surprisingly, many people inadvertently choose to fork their money over to Uncle Sam. Could it be that in a culture so obsessed with youth, old age is such a painful concept that some of us would rather throw our money down the drain than invest it for a more secure and comfortable future?

It's important to keep in mind that unlike dollars invested in insurance, money put toward retirement is not protection against emergencies or unforeseen disasters. None of us is getting any younger, and with the life expectancy projected to be eighty-one for men and eighty-six for women for people who are sixty-five in the year 2000, most of us are probably going to be around for a long time.[15] At the same time, the concepts of senior citizenship and retirement are undergoing some radical changes. Many people have no interest in retiring. Quite simply, they like their work and want to pursue it indefinitely. This is especially true of self-employed people who, over the years, have developed interests and work schedules that suit their particular wants and needs. Work to them is not something one does from nine to five, five days a week, but an essential part of a total lifestyle. Still, when people get older they often like to have the option of allowing themselves more time for leisure, or to pursue work that might have more intrinsic value but less financial reward. With the government offering such inviting inducements to put money into retirement plans, we have good reason to think of our later years as a time for exploring new options in our work and personal lives. With good health and enough money to live in comfort (if not luxury), this can be a rewarding and productive period in which to be alive.

Who qualifies for an IRA and/or Keogh?

As of 1982, virtually all workers are eligible for an IRA. This includes employees with or without pension plans at their companies, and self-employed individuals. Keoghs are available to any self-employed person who earns at least a portion of his income in this manner. Employees are eligible only for an IRA. If you are self-employed—full or part-time—you can open both an IRA and Keogh account.

How much money can you put into these funds?

You can contribute up to $2,000 a year to an IRA account. If you have a nonworking spouse, you can contribute an additional $250 a year. If both you and your spouse work, you can each contribute $2,000 to separate IRA accounts. In addition, if you are self-employed, you can now put as much as 25 percent of the monies you earned *through self-employment*, up to $30,000, in a Keogh account. As far as the government is concerned, there is no minimum amount that you can contribute to a retirement fund (though banks and other institutions can set their own guidelines). Also, you cannot compensate for a year in which you contributed little or no money by putting in more during another year. Each year is considered a separate entity.

Where can you invest your retirement dollars?

Basically, you can make the same kinds of investments with Keoghs and IRAs as in most other circumstances. Your money can be invested in bank accounts, stocks and bonds, real estate, insurance company products—virtually anything except commodities, options, coins, stamps, and works of art. The relative safety and potential return on your investment are no different for retirement plans. If you put your money in a bank C.D., for example, you may receive a lower return on your investment, but you know that money is safe. If, on the other hand, you invest your Keogh in high-risk stocks, both your profit potential and risk of loss increase considerably. You are also not obliged to put all your tax-deferred retirement eggs into one basket. You can put half of the money into a C.D., one-quarter into stocks, and one-quarter into real estate. You can also revise your investment formula each year. Remember: All profits accruing from these investments must be left in your retirement account, but they do earn interest.

When can you withdraw your money?

You can start taking money out of a tax-deferred retirement account at age fifty-nine and one-half, even if you haven't retired. You do not have to start withdrawing money until you are seventy. Should you decide to withdraw any of the money before age fifty-nine and one-half, you will be penalized 10 percent of the amount you withdraw, and that money will be subject to tax as income. This is not as severe at it might sound if you consider that after about five years the money usually has earned more interest than the combined penalty and tax bite.

Are there any other important considerations?

Because retirement accounts are being offered by so many different kinds of institutions, it pays to shop around. There can be major differences in potential profit, safety of principle, administration fees, and minimum contributions. If you want to get started, though, you can't go too far wrong with an insured C.D. account at a bank.

Contingencies:
TAKING CARE OF THE
"WHAT IFS"

THERE IS A CLASSIC SCENE IN WOODY ALLEN'S first movie, *Take the Money and Run*, in which prisoners who are being punished are sent to the "hole" along with a life insurance salesman. The implication being that the insurance agent's sales pitch is even more unbearable than the hell of solitary confinement.

Let's face it: Insurance isn't one of the fun topics of conversation. First of all, nobody ever likes to think about unpleasantries like illness, disability, or theft, much less take money from their day-to-day lives and spend it on things that seem so remote. Still, most of us know people who have suddenly become ill or were temporarily disabled by an accident. Employees are often covered against such eventualities by company-provided insurance policies. These are protective measures that workers in many industries demand as part of their employees' benefits package. Do freelancers need such protection any less? To the contrary. Anyone in their own business has much more to lose by not obtaining appropriate coverage.

To get a basic idea of your insurance needs, spend a few minutes thinking about the following questions:

- What areas out of my control require protective measures?

- What is my tolerance for risk versus my need for security?

- Do I have a concept of how I would handle the following unforeseen possibilities?

- Prolonged illness (including medical and hospital expenses)

- Fire or theft

- Long-term disability

- Obligations incurred by my family if I die

When you think about these contingencies, weigh the peace of mind that accrues when you know you are protected against these eventualities in relation to the expense involved. Also, keep in mind that insurance is never an all-or-nothing proposition. The rule of thumb is that the more you spend, the more coverage you can buy. In many instances, however, a modestly priced policy will suit your purposes.

Health Insurance

Did your mother ever encourage you to become a teacher or a civil servant because "they have a wonderful health plan"? Many of us who have never been seriously ill or stuck in a hospital bed for any length of time have a hard time relating to this kind of thinking. But the potential cost of such eventualities can wipe out even a fat nest egg. That's why financial advisors like Erna Ferris consider health insurance "as mandatory as the food you put on the table every day."

People who have never experienced any medical problems sometimes think that acknowledging their existence somehow increases the possibility of bringing them about, and there probably is something to be said for the notion that too much psychic energy invested in thoughts of illness can become almost as much of a problem as the infirmities themselves. But this is a rather one-sided approach to the issue. Some occurrences are—to a great extent—out of our control, no matter how well we care for ourselves or how healthy we've been in the past. That's why some type of health insurance is a must for self-employed individuals.

If you've recently left a full-time job, ask how long you can be covered by your former company's health plan. If your spouse is covered through his or her company, you might also be eligible. If you have to purchase your own health insurance, find out if you are eligible for a group plan either through a union or some professional association. It is also possible for two or more people to form their own group and receive lower rates.

When you evaluate how much coverage you need, consider your age, general health, and your anticipated medical requirements. If, for example, you are young, single, and in good health, you might opt for an insurance plan with a higher *deductible* than an older person with a history of illness. Deductibles are simply the amount you must pay before the coverage goes into effect.

Before you decide to buy any kind of insurance policy, be sure to shop around. In the case of health insurance, however, you might want to stick with Blue Cross and Blue Shield if their rates are competitive. "They're the biggest and the best," notes David Feinstein, "and the easiest to collect from." Depending on your specific medical needs, however, other companies can sometimes offer a better deal. Some policies, for example, have better coverage for psychotherapists; others allow more toward dental expenses. Another kind of health insurance that makes sense for some freelancers is a prepaid health plan. This means that your premium covers any and all medical expenses you might incur. If you need frequent medical attention, this kind of program might work best for you. The following checklist can help you select the most appropriate health coverage.

Things to Look For	Things to Ask Yourself
The best rate	Have I checked all possible sources for the best deal, including my former employer, my spouse's policy, unions, professional associations, forming groups with other freelancers?
Differences in deductible	Will it ultimately cost me more if I pay less for a policy with a higher deductible?
Extent of coverage	What is my medical history? How much have I spent for medical services during the past few years? What are my family's needs?
Type of coverage	Does the policy cover the kinds of medical expenses my family and I are likely to require?

Disability Insurance

If you accept the need for some kind of health insurance as something worthy of inclusion in your budget, you might also want to consider a disability policy. Let's say you've invested in a comprehensive medical and hospitalization plan that takes care of the bulk of potential expenses from virtually any medical emergency. You are still liable to lose a substantial amount of money if you can't work while you are sick. Remember that many of your basic expenses will still be mounting up while you're unable to work. What to do?

"I believe that all self-employed individuals should have disability income," says David Feinstein. "If your freelance income is dependent on your work time, nobody is going to compensate you if you become sick or get hit by a truck. So I believe that freelancers should invest in themselves by taking out as much disability income as they can possibly afford. Freelancers with a heavy overhead should also look into a BOE (business overhead expense) policy which covers some of your operating expenses should you become disabled. A BOE is based upon the amount of income you generate and covers things like your office and secretary."

In spite of the logic of investing in a disability policy, our panel of experts agree that few freelancers have this kind of coverage. "Very few self-employed people are able to show us how they would live if they didn't work for six months," says Erna Ferris. "That's why I feel that disability is as essential as a health insurance policy."

If you decide to investigate the various disability policies, you will find a wide range of prices and coverage. Some policies pay your expenses plus a set amount of money for every day that you are unable to work, while others simply cover your fixed expenses. As with any kind of insurance, shop around carefully to get the most coverage for the least amount of money. Find out if your union, professional association, or college alumni organization offer any kind of program. Ask your accountant how much coverage you need and where you should buy it. Disability insurance is worth thinking about. At the very least, ask yourself how you would get by if you could not work for an extended period of time.

Theft and Fire Insurance

If you live in a large urban area, you probably know that burglaries are so common that some people leave a twenty dollar bill on a table near the door so that when they walk in, they'll know immediately whether their apartment has been ripped off. We know freelancers who have invested thousands of dollars in elaborate security systems and still feel vulnerable. Aside from the value of the stolen property, there is a particularly horrendous feeling that accompanies the discovery that someone has been in our private space ransacking our drawers and defiling our personal effects.

If your property is ever burglarized or ravaged by fire, it's going to be a horrendous experience—insurance or no insurance. The least you can do for yourself is to cover the financial end of this disaster. Since you are only paying for the amount of protection necessary to cover your potential losses, the annual nut for fire and theft insurance can be kept down. For example, you can currently buy $5,000 worth of coverage for about $50 a year (or less than $1 per week). As the value of your property grows, you can simply buy more coverage at a proportionate price. A number of these policies include coverage for robbery (of your person) and liability (somebody hurts themselves on your property) for the same low price.

A good place to start pricing fire and theft insurance is through the federal government (Federal Crime Insurance, P.O. Box 41033, Washington, D.C. 20014). Insurance brokers can write these policies, although we have found some companies that offer comparable rates and whose coverage also includes fire and liability. But while some companies might turn you down if you live in a "high-risk" neighborhood, the federal government must provide coverage (their only requirement is a "dead bolt" lock and one of several types of window locks). Incidentally, if you run your business in a more rural area with a low crime rate, you still want to consider protecting yourself against fires and other natural disasters.

When it comes to insuring your property, virtually every expert suggests that you do so immediately. Considering the outlay of money versus the protection you are getting, there really aren't many good reasons to risk the consequences that might ensue if you don't invest in this kind of insurance policy. Still,

117

there are differences between the kinds of coverage you can buy. Here are a few things to look for:

▶ *Deductible.* Many policies pay you after the first $100 of loss. You can often save money on your premium payments by purchasing a policy with a higher deductible—say $250.

▶ If you have items of particular vintage or value, be sure that you are insured for the replacement value of that item. For example, an antique clock can easily be worth five times as much as a new one. Unless its value as an antique is specified in the policy, the insurance company will invariably depreciate the clock as if its age decreased its value.

▶ Certain items—such as cash and jewelry—might not be covered or only given limited coverage on some policies.

▶ Some policies provide money for a place to stay if your premises are ravaged by fire.

Life Insurance

If you are single, there is a good chance that you don't need any life insurance whatsoever. But if you have a family, or plan to, you might want to give it some consideration.

"I believe that people should be responsible for themselves," says Erna Ferris, "and that includes taking care of any obligations that remain after their death." If you're married, your spouse is responsible for all outstanding debts, including taxes.

You ought to have at least enough life insurance to cover those kinds of obligations.

Even financial consultants who are not very strong on life insurance recommend it for those who are married. "I believe in it when you have someone who is going to benefit from it—namely a wife and children," says David Feinstein, "but I don't recommend it for anyone who is not married." If you think you might need life insurance in the foreseeable future, you would do well to understand some fundamentals.

There are two basic kinds of life insurance. The first type is called *term* (also known as ordinary or straight life). With this kind of insurance, you pay a yearly fee, which increases periodically as you get older. The second type is known as *whole* life. In this case, you are paying not only for the coverage, but also into a kind of forced savings plan that allows you to receive money if you cash the policy in (this is called the *cash redemption value* of the policy).

Insurance salespeople may try to sell you a whole life policy based on the savings aspect it offers. In general, though, the interest you are earning is less than if you put the difference between a whole and term life policy into a high-interest money market account. Most financial experts who don't specialize in insurance feel that whole life isn't the way for most people to go. "Don't buy [a whole life policy]," counsels Andrew Tobias. "Insurance salesmen are very eager to sell whole life policies because their commissions are so much higher than on term policies. [And that, in turn] is because the insurance company's profits are so much higher."[16]

If you are wondering where to look for the best deals on your term insurance policies, the answer is pretty much the same as with health and disability insurance. The best rates can be found through employee groups, unions, or professional associations. If you can't hook into one of these plans, look into savings banks that offer life insurance policies called "Savings Bank Life Insurance," or "SBLI." At this writing, only a few states offer SBLI, but if you have a relative living in one of those states, he or she might be able to apply for you. If all else fails, allow a number of brokers (preferably ones that deal with more than one company) to design a policy that best suits your needs. Remember, life insurance rates can vary anywhere from 50 to 100 percent, so it is particularly important that you shop around.

A Brief Word About Wills

A will is nothing more than a legal document that indicates how you want your property to be distributed after you've gone. A will ensures that your property will be passed on in accordance with your wishes. Otherwise, your property will pass in accordance with the laws of the state in which you reside. Say you want to leave all your estate to your spouse and the laws of your state maintain that—barring a will to the contrary—all property is to be distributed equally among a deceased person's spouse and children, then your spouse would only receive part of your property. If, on the other hand, you want your estate distributed according to state laws, you don't need to have a will drawn up.

Since most of us work very hard to accumulate what property we have, it behooves us to consider who is going to get that property after we're gone. Here are some key points to keep in mind:

○ You may be able to draw up a will without hiring an attorney, but to do so, you must know the laws of the state in which you reside.

○ Laws differ from state to state as to the legal requirements necessary to draw up a will in regard to (among other things): the number of witnesses that must be present when the will is signed; the need to have the will notarized; and whether certain people can be totally excluded from the will. In some states, for example, the spouse is entitled to at least one-third of the estate no matter what.

○ Don't just assume that the state will distribute your property equitably among your surviving relatives. Find out what the laws are and, within those boundaries, have a will drawn up that clearly indicates who gets what.

○ If you have no surviving relatives and die without a will, your property will pass to the state.

NET WORTH

JON, A FREELANCE GRAPHIC DESIGNER, WAS CONtemplating starting his own design studio. He was discussing it over dinner at his house with a colleague, Anne. Anne noticed the table Jon had was an antique. "Yes, I got it from my wife's family. It's an heirloom," he told her. Anne said, "I used to have a lot of this kind of furniture in my house when I was growing up. You know, with the two chairs, this furniture is worth way over $10,000." Possessions such as Jon's add nicely to your net worth. When you go to the bank to ask for a loan, remembering this could be helpful.

Net worth—what's that? Actually, it is a financial picture of who you are today. It's arrived at by using a balance sheet—a sheet that balances your assets (what you own) and your liabilities (what you owe). When you subtract your liabilities from your assets, you arrive at your net worth. It takes some time to figure out, but you gain valuable knowledge from it.

NET WORTH

Some freelancers discover they are worth a lot more than they think.

Knowledge of the value of your assets can help you decide how much insurance to get on personal property. When figuring the value of antiques, art, jewelry, or collector items, you'll need to get an appraisal. Also check with your accountant to see if you've included all the important items that pertain to you. As with budgeting, many freelancers are surprised once they see the figures in black and white. They often discover they are worth more than they think.

YOUR BALANCE SHEET

Assets—What You Own

CASH

—money on hand
—savings accounts
—checking accounts
—other bank accounts
—

INVESTMENTS

—stocks
—bonds
—other
—
—IRA
—Keogh
—other retirement plan
—real estate
—annuities
—other
—
—

PROPERTY

—furniture
—house
—antiques
—jewelry
—clothing
—other

OTHER

—
—

Liabilities—What You Owe

BILLS

—rent
—mortgage
—utilities
—insurance
—credit cards
—loans
  —auto
  —home improvement
  —other
—anticipated taxes
—average monthly
  out-of-pocket expenses

PRIVATE DEBTS

—
—
—

OTHER

—
—
—
—
—
—
—
—

TOTAL ASSETS   TOTAL LIABILITIES

ASSETS:
MINUS LIABILITIES: _____

EQUALS NET WORTH: _____

CHECKLIST FOR GAINING FINANCIAL CONTROL ✔

CATEGORY	HAVE	WILL GET SOON	THINKING ABOUT IT	NOT A PRIORITY
1) EXPENSE RECORDS				
2) INCOME RECORDS				
3) BUDGET				
4) SAVINGS—CUSHION				
5) SAVINGS—SEPARATE ACCOUNTS				
6) INSURANCE a) HEALTH				
b) DISABILITY				
c) LIFE				
d) FIRE AND THEFT AND LIABILITY				
7) RETIREMENT				
8) WILL				
9) ANTICIPATED TAX FUND				
10) FINANCIAL TEAM a) ACCOUNTANT				
b) LAWYER				
c) BANKER				
d) INSURANCE AGENT				
11) NET WORTH (ASSETS MINUS LIABILITIES)				

4

SUCCESS: What You Want and How to Get It

As Bob Dylan says in one of his songs, "Everybody's doing something." But to what end? When we ask self-employed people this question, the answer we most often get is: "to be successful." Further probing of this issue usually indicates that many of the same individuals who say they are striving for success have never really gotten clear about what this crucial concept means to them. We believe that if you are going to take a road, you ought to know where that road is going to lead (or at least where you would like it to lead). That's why we asked people to tell us what success meant to them. Here is a sampling of the answers we received:

DEFINITIONS OF SUCCESS

☆   "Money, a lot of money."

☆   "To be happy."

☆ "The ability to make a dream come true."

☆ "Finding a niche for yourself."

☆ "Feeling you belong for ten minutes."

☆ "Doing what you want and having the world reward you for it by paying you well."

☆ "Making a lot of money doing something you love to do."

☆ "Being viable and paying your way."

☆ "Staying true to your purpose."

☆ "Nurturing yourself by what you are doing."

☆ "To win a Pulitzer prize. . . . Come to think of it, that probably wouldn't make me feel successful either."

☆ "To be acknowledged by my peers as being very good at what I do."

☆ "Making it . . . you achieve your goals."

☆ "Success is not necessarily monetary. You're happy with what you're doing and the state of life you've reached."

☆ "Making a reasonable living doing something you enjoy."

☆ "Having a good relationship with my husband. Having good family relationships and a career that's satisfying and profitable."

What does success mean to you: money, fame, notoriety, respect, spiritual peace, emotional happiness? As you can see from the diverse concepts people have of success, there are many sides to this question. However, the one factor that pops us most often when people in our culture define success is *money*. On some level, a person with $10 million has a magical quality for the rest of us. There are those who would go so far as to say that it doesn't matter so much if that money was inherited, won in a lottery, extorted in some quasilegal scam, or earned through the most high-minded endeavor. The only thing that matters is whether or not you've got it. If you do, you're an important, charismatic individual. If you don't, you're worthless—a *loser*.

Frankly, we can't *buy* this limited notion of success—not that we don't believe in making as much money as possible, all other things being equal. As you may have noticed, however, all other things are rarely—if ever—equal. For example, we don't consider a multimillionaire with a bleeding ulcer successful (though he is unquestionably more successful than a pauper with a bleeding ulcer). We also don't consider successful anyone who has gotten where he or she is without maintaining some sense of ethical values and emotional balance. It would be much easier to view success from strictly a dollars and cents point of view (your accountant could go over your books and let you know how you're doing). Bringing in personal and emotional issues opens up a whole other can of beans—but it is one we had better open if we want to know what our meal is going to taste like once it is prepared. Don't misunderstand: We're all in favor of you making as much money and gaining as much notoriety as you possibly can. We just want you to spend a little time exploring your feelings about success so that when your proverbial ship comes in, you can be both rich *and* happy. With this in mind, we'd like to offer our own definition of success: **the process of achieving all the possibilities in one's work and personal life that one is capable of.**

Let's take a moment to digest this view of success. In defining success as a *process*, we are indicating that it is not only something one strives for in the distant future, but also a way of conducting one's life *right now*. We are also treating work and personal life as connected, rather than discrete, parts of one's being. It is not uncommon for a person to believe that his work life is going well while his personal life is falling apart at the seams, yet recent studies have indicated that even people who work nine-to-five cannot fully compartmentalize the important areas of their lives. In other words, the studies tell us, there isn't really any such thing as "leaving your troubles at the office." How much stronger, then, is the connection between a freelancer's work and personal life? For most of us, there is a delicate balance between these two areas that must be maintained if emotional peace is not to be sacrificed in the name of being a success in business.

One of the most extreme examples of abandoning all sense of personal values in the name of "good business" can be found in the movie *The Godfather*. There is one memorable scene where a gang member who has defected to a rival organization is being "taken for a ride." After pleading for his life to no avail, he says: "Tell Mike [the man who ordered his death] that I always liked him, it was only business." To which another gang leader replies, "Mike understands that, he always liked you a lot too."

We're not trying to say that these characters' problems revolve around erroneous or incomplete concepts of success. Like many other people in above-board enterprises, the characters in *The Godfather* mistakenly believed that the rest of their lives could be magically separated from their work.

WHO ARE THE TRULY SUCCESSFUL PEOPLE?

WE'VE NOTED THAT SUCCESS IS NOT SIMPLE TO DE-fine and, therefore, not simple to achieve. Many of us are walking around with notions of success that have not been carefully considered, or that are based more on what our family or peer group tells us they should be rather than on our own values and inner feelings. Our society has fostered erroneous notions of success that many of us carry around. One of the most common notions revolves around the myth that success and happiness are equated with becoming a star in some phase of show business. No matter how many headlines of suicides or quasisuicides by the Freddie Prinzes, the Elvis Presleys, Janis Joplins, or John Belushis make the front pages, people can't seem to accept that they wouldn't be a lot happier with tons of money and notoriety. They are certain that they could handle it with no problem, but experts like Dr. Martha Friedman—author of *Overcoming the Fear of Success* and therapist to many famous people in the arts—believe that a sudden windfall of money and adulation can often create more problems than it solves. She told us:

"The equation for happiness in our culture is [supposed to be] money, fame and recognition. Of course, that's not really so. I'm not saying that people with a lot of

"It all started when he made the best-seller list."

129

money are generally unhappy. On the contrary . . . most of us feel more secure with a lot of money. But many people who suddenly come into a lot of money don't know what to do with it . . . in some way, they feel that they don't deserve this success and try to sabotage it. [In extreme cases] the person feels so guilty about his success that he thinks someone is going to kill him. So, he goes home and kills himself."

Dr. Friedman believes that the key to handling success is the ability to *integrate* those good things that happen to you into your overall scheme. Successful people are able to "go with the flow." They are equally adept at solving unforeseen problems that come their way and handling unexpected good fortune. Men and women who are genuinely successful project a kind of ease in coordinating different aspects of their lives. This doesn't mean that they don't go through periods of stress from time to time; we are all subject to ups and downs in our work and personal lives. The critical difference is that successful people seem to roll with the punches and rarely get thrown off course. Let's explore some of the major attributes that together form a profile of success.

Nine Attributes Successful People Have in Common

1. High levels of self-esteem

Author Truman Capote was fond of saying that "more grief has been caused by answered prayers than by unanswered prayers." Essentially, this means that many people have more emotional problems after the very things they have been striving for become real. Successful people do not have such problems. They are certain that they deserve their success. When it comes, they know how to embrace it and are not prone to undermining it. Another way of putting it is that they like themselves enough to feel that they are entitled to any and all good things that come their way.

The other side of the self-esteem coin is that those people who like themselves enough to embrace success also know how to put setbacks into perspective. Everyone sometimes experiences rejection and other losses, but there are differences in how we regard them. Instead of perceiving setbacks as signs of defeat or personal failure, successful individuals tend to regard them as temporary situations that will eventually be resolved. Dr. Adele Scheele, career coach and author of the book *Skills for Success*, puts the issue into perspective by comparing the search for success to fishing:

> "If you think of life as a test of your self-worth, that's a lousy way to live. If, instead, you think of life as an experiment, you try different things and see what works for you. If something works, great! You say: 'Hey, this worked; let's see what else works.' If it doesn't work, you try something else. If something doesn't work for you, that doesn't mean you're a failure. . . . [Finding success] is really nothing more than an experimental process. . . . It's kind of like hunting or fishing where you can't say you failed. You can just say that you didn't catch anything and cast your line in again."

2.   Reliance on gut feelings

Successful people have good instincts, whether their area of expertise is baseball, computers, or one of the arts. Part of these instincts relate to innate talents that are necessary to become

Sometimes your gut feelings tell you not to take a job.

outstanding in certain fields. But more often than not, good instincts are acquired through years of experience. To say that a person trusts his instincts or gut feelings is another way of saying that he is a confident decision maker.

Whenever you make a decision, some time has to elapse before the results become apparent. In some cases, the effect of an important decision can have an impact for a long time to come. Successful people do not become overwhelmed by the ramifications of their decisions. They confidently evaluate all the data at hand and call the shots as they see them.

Why is it that some people seem to consistently make correct decisions, while others invariably make wrong ones? Luck may play a part in solving this riddle, but such luck is rarely blind. People who trust their gut feelings understand that far from being random, good luck comes to those who do what they can to control their own destinies. Sometimes making the right decision means going against the opinions of others, overcoming your own doubts, and following your gut feelings. Let's take a case in point:

Fred had been struggling as a singer-songwriter for a number of years. He hadn't had much luck, but understood that he was in a highly competitive area in which success rarely came overnight. Still, he was anxious to get "the show on the road," as he put it. After several months of sending around his most recent demo tape, he received an offer from a manager. Although this manager had launched several successful careers, he was known as someone who exploited talented people. Fred recognized that the offer the manager was making him was unfair. Still, he wanted to advance his career to the next level. The members of his band encouraged Fred to take the deal. "After all," they pointed out, "this is the only offer we've had."

Fred gave the matter careful consideration. He remembered a time in the past when he accepted an offer he felt was unfair. The result was that although a good deal of money was made, Fred was cheated out of almost all of it. After that incident, he felt strongly that he would have been better off not entering into any kind of agreement that would lead to his being exploited. Now this offer was being flashed in front of his nose. Would it be better to take it and forget about his feeling that he was probably going to get exploited again, or would it be better to turn it down and continue looking for a better situation. In spite of all the arguments from his band, Fred decided that he would feel very badly about himself if he went against his gut feeling that this was not a good situation. "If I ignore the lessons I've learned in the past, I'm denying the validity of my own experiences," he reasoned. Fred called up the manager and said: "Thanks, but your offer is unsatisfactory. I'll have to turn it down." In making his decision, Fred demonstrated a good deal of trust in himself. He understood the difficulties involved in generating another offer, but he made the choice based on courage rather than fear.

He had enough faith in his gut feelings to do what he believed best.

3.   The burning desire to achieve goals

. . . it is not given to me to know how many steps
are necessary to reach my goal. Failure I may encounter
at the thousandth step, yet success lies behind the next bend
in the road. Never will I know how close it lies
until I turn the corner.

Og Mandino[1]

For every inspirational story of someone who overcame seemingly insurmountable obstacles on the road to success, there are ten stories of men and women who had all the odds stacked in their favor but got derailed by the smallest hindrance. How badly do *you* want to reach those goals that underlie your success? If your desire isn't very strong, perhaps you ought to rethink your goals. People who feel strongly about what they want and are willing to do what it takes to get there have already won a good part of the battle.

When you start laying out the steps needed to achieve your goals, it is easy to become overwhelmed. Aside from all the competition out there, you will have your own internal obstacles to deal with. There will be days when it seems virtually impossible to make any real progress, nights when you ask yourself if you've bitten off more than you can chew. But if you are truly motivated, you won't get derailed. People who are wishy-washy about what they are after often let their dreams drown in a puddle (never mind a flood), whereas successful individuals look at every obstacle in their path as a challenge they must overcome to move closer to success. It's not that they don't get discouraged from time to time; they do. The thing that sets them apart is their determination to push on until they get what they're after.

4. The ability to take action in the face of doubt and fear

Have you ever started a project and then abandoned it because you ran into some unforeseen problems that made you anxious? Anybody who attempts anything is bound to run into some kind of snag or impasse at one time or another. The critical difference is how one handles these difficulties. Successful people are ready to sacrifice a temporary feeling of comfort or security in order to achieve their goals. They understand that a full commitment means pushing through emotions like doubt, fear, and anxiety. Less committed individuals often allow such emotions to stop them midstream. The feeling is: "Why should I keep working so hard at this when there is a good chance that I'll never reach my goal?" Ironically, psychologists like Rollo May have concluded that supposedly negative emotions like doubt and anxiety are actually important components of success:

> It is the seeming contradiction that we must be fully committed, but we also must be aware at the same time that we might possibly be wrong. This dialectic relationship between conviction and doubt is characteristic of the highest types of courage. . . . Commitment is healthiest when it is not without doubt, but in spite of doubt.[2]

You may recall that in Chapter Two we emphasized the importance of following through on your decisions and plans by doing those things you've committed to do. You always want to remain flexible enough to change your plans if it becomes necessary, but you don't want to get sidetracked every time you become anxious. Dr. Martha Friedman believes that the only solution to such stifling emotions is to keep on pushing through:

"People often tell me that they can't work because they feel panic. They say: 'It doesn't feel good; I'm very [anxious] and I don't know why.' I tell them: 'Don't stop and try to figure out why. Just keep on doing the task. Your feelings of panic [and anxiety] will decrease while you are working.'"

5. Knowing when and where to look for feedback

All of us need the input of others to let us know if we're headed in the right direction. For the self-employed person who doesn't have the kind of built-in network that corporations provide, the feedback must come from a team that the individual creates for himself. Most experienced freelancers have peers and mentors to

"Come on, what do you really think of this last chapter?"

bounce ideas off, but some ideas are so innovative that even the most trusted consultants cannot comprehend their brilliance. Another problem may arise when someone with unfulfilled ambitions in your field responds negatively, for personal reasons, instead of offering you a well-considered opinion of your work. And finally, there are those times when your idea really isn't all that good and you might be too close to it to accept criticism.

Successful people know where to go for feedback and have the wherewithal to make the best use of it. Many a brilliant project has been turned around by a relatively minor suggestion. But here again, you have to rely on your gut instincts. Do you respect the person who is evaluating your work? Does his or her criticism ring true to you? Are you getting a similar response from a number of sources? Is there a change or two you can make to improve the quality or value of your work?

There are no simple answers beyond developing a reliable feedback network and the good judgment for how to best incorporate it in your work.

6. Being an effective planner

We've discussed the importance of good planning in previous sections as a major component of reaching your goals. In observing the particulars of how successful people plan, research psychologist Charles A. Garfield came to the following conclusions:

> "While their peers tend to be consumed primarily with short term gains, [successful individuals] are much more likely to channel their energies into long-term planning. They decide in advance what skills, financial resources . . . and equipment are required to do the job well; less productive individuals often launch into a mission zealously and then discover, deep into the project, that a major change of course is required, sometimes at great expense."[3]

Successful people tend to create positive solutions to obstacles instead of changing their plans midstream. There are no set rules about how long to stick to a plan before changing course, but we have seen too many self-employed people get discouraged too easily instead of seeing things through. Often, these individuals impulsively decide to pursue a goal without taking the time to find out what steps are required and how long they are likely to take. Then, when they hit a snag, poor planners switch to another goal at the very moment when they ought to be digging in harder than ever. This is unfortunate, because success is more likely to come to those who feel strongly about what they want, formulate an effective plan of how to get it, and do whatever it takes to see that plan to fruition.

7.   Having an inner sense of confidence

[Successful individuals] have an internal focus
of control, and thus their sense of fulfillment comes
primarily from within. Their less successful colleagues are
much more externally controlled and heavily
dependent on outside validation.

Charles Garfield[4]

What means more to you—praise from others or the knowledge that you've done something well? We all need approval at times. But in regard to work, successful people are more concerned with competence than approval, or as Dr. Martha Friedman puts it: "They don't need to look for love in the wrong places. . . . They want to know they're good rather than being told that they're good." It is this inner feeling of confidence that allows successful people to forge ahead in their work. On the other hand, less successful individuals are often stifled by negative criticism or even the anticipation of such a response. Ironically, this lack of confidence is often telegraphed to others and colors their response. Confident people, on the other hand, tend to create a center of positive energy which attracts and influences others.

So what we have here is a two-edged sword. Those same people who have little need for outside validation often create an atmosphere that nurtures this kind of approval. On the contrary, people who are desperately seeking approval are far less likely to get it. Nobody is certain whether this irony is the function of some kind of reverse psychology or some quirk in human nature. But a highly successful attorney recently offered an apt, if somewhat cynical, explanation of this dynamic:

"Basically, people are insecure about themselves and their opinions. When they sense that you really believe in what you are saying or doing, they are drawn to you. If they feel that you're insecure, it mirrors their own insecurity and they quickly get turned off. Someone once said: 'When you project confidence in what you are doing, you become a genius in the eyes of those around you. But when you seem insecure or wishy-washy, people think you don't know what you're talking about.'"

8. Creating your own luck

We've all read about the actress who becomes an "overnight sensation" after struggling and almost starving for much of her career. After years of—as they say in show business—"not being able to get arrested," the media is now pining for the most minute details of her personal life: "Miss so-and-so," reporters ask with awe in their voices, "how did you become such a great success?" After spending most of the past ten years out of work, the actress hardly knows what to say. "Hang in there," she counsels, most impressed with the originality of her advice. "If you have a dream, stick with it, and you'll get where you're trying to go." As she mouths these well-worn truisms, the actress remembers a missed opportunity six years earlier that almost launched her into stardom. She also reflects that without a few recent breaks, she might still be one of many talented, but starving, performers. Now that she's crossed that invisible line between obscurity and fame, however, people who once had no interest in her whatsoever are hanging on to her every word.

The actress understands—as do most successful people—that even though the world around her perceives enormous differences, there really are only small differences between her and the other talented but less successful people in the same field. Perhaps she was just a bit more aggressive in selling herself, or a little more focused on what she was after. Maybe it was nothing more than plain good luck. But never make the mistake of thinking that luck is completely random.

Successful individuals mention luck as a determining factor at least as often as other people. The critical difference is that those who don't succeed see themselves as victims of bad luck, while those who do usually are creators of good luck. Put another way: *Successful individuals focus on those things that are within their control while others tend to dwell on things they cannot control.*

In viewing success as a number of skills anyone can master, career counselor Adele Scheele cites two clichés that people sometimes use to explain their lack of luck and, conversely, the good fortune of others:

● "It's not what you know but who you know." Do you think most successful people got where they are because they had a relative who set them up? There are examples of nepotism in many fields, but most truly successful people did not get where they are through the influence of a highly placed relative. This doesn't mean, however, that they didn't have connections. Although they might not be able to verbalize it, successful individuals learned how to use the people they know as contacts and meet new people who could help them connect in the future. To put it another way: Successful people create and utilize success teams or networks. Did you ever consider that if you utilize all the contacts you already have among your friends, relatives, and business associates, you are probably no more than three steps away from the most powerful people in any field. Do you make the most out of this fantastic network of human resources or do you dwell on how unfair life is because you don't have an uncle in a powerful position in your chosen field?

Adele Scheele says that "fairness is an artificial measure that's made up by school, but nothing in life is fair." In school everyone is supposed to have an equal chance to excel, so it's not surprising that people often expect other situations to work the same way. In reality, we are not born with equal abilities, nor are we presented with equal or fair opportunities. Successful people know how to make the best of those opportunities that come their way. If they don't have the contacts necessary to accomplish a particular goal, successful people are out there developing them. They certainly don't waste time groaning about how unfair the world is.

● "You were in the right place at the right time." Some people view their more successful counterparts as having had better luck in their timing. More often than not, though, such apparent strokes of good fortune are the result of perseverance and hard work.

Let's return for a moment to our friend the actress, who, after ten lean years, became an "overnight success." This is the stuff headlines in *People* magazine are made of. It feeds into many of our fantasies to think that we can just drop in when we are so inclined and magically get discovered. Oh, things like this do happen once in a great, great while. But most people who are in the right place at the right time have often been trying to make it for years, or as Adele Scheele puts it:

"Most people who find themselves in the right place at the right time also had many experiences being at the wrong place at the right time and the right place at the

WRONG PLACE / RIGHT TIME

RIGHT PLACE / WRONG TIME

RIGHT PLACE / RIGHT TIME

wrong time. It's not just persistence that gets them over the hump, but trying again in new and different ways."

The "new and different ways" that successful people try are an important key to creating luck. The important thing is the understanding that luck is something we all have a hand in creating. There are always going to be certain factors we cannot control, but if you feel you haven't had any good luck, ask yourself this: *Am I doing everything I can about those things that are within my control?* If the answer is *no*, ask yourself what you can do to create a better climate in which luck can flourish.

9.   Being a well-integrated person

If you look at a truly successful individual, not only will you find many of the attributes we have been discussing, you will also note that in the largest sense, the whole person is much more than a mere sum of individual components. This is truly the key to sizing up your own success and that of others. This book's primary focus is to help you become successful business people, but as we have said previously, a fat bank account and a lot of work coming in are not necessarily synonymous with success. We would like you to take a look at the people you would choose as role models for success. Do they have a lot of money? Are they respected in their line of work and by the community at large? Are they people with rich family lives and friendships, and perhaps most importantly, do they seem happy with themselves?

We strongly believe that there are few greater tragedies than a person whose success makes him unhappy. From our point of view, such an individual is not a true success. In conducting our seminars and consultations, we have discovered that people are hungry for answers, yet they often have not arrived at the right questions to ask. One of the most frequently asked questions is: "How do I become a success?" To which we answer: *"Do you *know what you mean by success? Have you stopped to think about everything that goes into being a success?"* These are the underlying questions that we strongly suggest you consider in shaping the direction you mold your integrated business/personal life. With this in mind, we have structured the following questionnaire to help bring these issues into focus for you. Some of the questions do not lend themselves to quick answers. We hope they will stimulate you to consider the most relevant factors determining your idea of business and personal success and assist you in asking more meaningful questions.

SUCCESS QUESTIONNAIRE

1. **What does success mean to me?** . . . .

2. **What part of that is financial success?** . . . .

3. **Where does personal life fit in?** . . . .

4. **What am I willing to sacrifice to achieve success?** . . . .

5. **What rewards do I anticipate from success?** . . . .

6. **Are the rewards worth what I'll have to go through to get them?** . . . .

7. **Do I have conflicts that keep me from pursuing success 100 percent?** . . . .

8. **How can I resolve these conflicts?** . . . .

9. **Are my ideas of success well thought out?** . . . .

10. **How has peer pressure influenced my ideas of success?** . . . .

11. **How has societal pressure influenced my ideas of success?** . . . .

12. **How has my family influenced my ideas of success?** . . . .

13. **What other factors have influenced my ideas of success?** . . . .

14. **How?** . . . .

15. **Write a one-paragraph statement of where you "see" yourself ten years from now. What notions of success does this statement embody?**

5

HABITS: The Mechanics of Doing

THE IMPORTANCE OF DEVELOPING GOOD HABITS

> The only difference between those who have
> failed and those who have succeeded lies in the
> difference of their habits. Good habits are the key to all
> success. Bad habits are the unlocked door to
> failure. Therefore, if I must be a slave to habit, let me
> be a slave to good habits.[1]
>
> Og Mandino

Now that you have given some thought to where you would
like to go in your business and personal life, ask yourself how

much effort you are willing to put forth in order to get there. Discussing success as a philosophical question is one thing, but taking the steps that lead you in the right direction is quite another. There may be worlds out there for you to conquer before you feel like a true success. But if you are like many freelancers, the greatest conquests involve overcoming your self-defeating habits. In and of themselves, habits—patterns of behavior acquired by frequent repetition—are mostly neutral. They can only be evaluated by the way they affect your life. Here is a case in point:

A self-employed bookkeeper named Paul described his typical day this way: "I get up at eleven o'clock most mornings, eat a leisurely breakfast and read the newspaper for a couple of hours, work for three or four hours, watch the six o'clock news, eat dinner, go out for drinks with my friends, come home and watch some late-night TV and get to sleep around three." In order to evaluate the habits that make up Paul's lifestyle, consider the following:

■ Paul has a business goal of increasing his income by 50 percent this year.

■ The best time to reach people he needs to contact is between nine and eleven in the morning.

■ Paul indicates that he has many creative ideas for increasing his number of clients late at night. During those hours he is usually glued to the TV and he doesn't bother to jot down his ideas.

It wouldn't exactly be going out on a limb to say that this freelancer's habits are not serving him well.

If only habits were more like automobiles, we could simply trade in our old, broken-down ones for some sleek new models. If only! Oh, well. It's kind of like that old joke that starts out saying, "I've got bad news and good news." The bad news is that when you decide to change your habits for the better, you've got to be prepared to come face to face with that part of your emotional baggage that bogs you down and holds you back. After all, it probably took many years to establish your current habits, so you can't very well expect to change them overnight. The good news is that there are things you can do *right now* to start changing those tired old habits of yours. The first step in trading in your self-defeating habits is to look at them simply as behaviors you would like to alter, rather than as indelible parts of your personality that must be defended at all costs.

Did you ever have a friend who successfully quit smoking cigarettes? Chances are that person first accepted that he had a habit that was endangering his health. In sharp contrast, there are other smokers who will argue for hours that cigarettes aren't really bad for you at all, or that the urban air that many of us breathe has more harmful substances than a pack of cigarettes. Why then should they give up smoking? People who separate those habits that prevent them from reaching their goals—be they personal, work, or health related—and treat them as behaviors that can be altered have taken an important first step toward positive change. Remember: *Your habits are nothing more than part of the picture of who you are today based on the past, just as your attempts to change those habits will help shape the person you become in the future.*

Where are you now in relation to your habits?

1. List five habits that enhance your chances for success.

2. List five habits that are holding you back from achieving all you can.

3. What obstacles do you see to changing the nonserving habits?

4. How can you overcome these obstacles?

5. When you run into obstacles, do you become discouraged and give up, or do you take a deep breath and attempt to meet the challenge at hand?

6. Are you focused on what you need to do to improve your situation, or do you place that responsibility on others?

7. Are you typically resistant to change?

8. Do you act on suggestions that would improve relevant areas of your life?

9. When you make a decision, do you allow enough time to achieve results?

10. Do you proceed in a step-by-step manner in the pursuit of your goals, or do you go about it in a haphazard manner?

Today's Freelancer: A Modern Samurai

There was a time not so very long ago when most mental health professionals believed that the only way to change habits was to help people discover the root of their self-defeating behaviors. In recent years, however, there has been a shift in emphasis from analyzing the past to dealing effectively with the present. Much of this thinking has its basis in Eastern philosophies like Zen, which began exerting a strong influence on the Human Potential Movement during the sixties. Here are five concepts of Zen which relate to the principles of successful freelancing:

 "Zen is simply a method of learning, of observing and of experiencing what you do every day . . . [it is] a practical discipline."

- "A goal of Zen is to realize your potential as a human being."

- "Zen is a philosophy of willpower. . . . You are saddled with the responsibility for yourself."

- "Zen is based on self-reliance. . . . You must learn to depend on yourself."

- "Zen wants you to act now, to experience this moment right now, directly. The effect of such action is to give you the power to cope [effectively]."

All these quotes come from the introduction to a book that was written almost five hundred years ago by a samurai warrior

A freelancer must know when to attack.

named Miyamoto Musashi.[2] But what does today's free-lancer—consumed as he or she is with mundane matters like paying the rent and meeting deadlines—have in common with the samurai of ancient Japan? More than you might think. Like these warriors of old, the contemporary freelancer must be able to sell his services to the powers that be. He must be self-reliant so that he can forge his own path. He must learn to develop patience so that he doesn't become frustrated. He must develop the instincts to know when to attack and the wisdom to know when to rest. Though times have changed radically in many ways, the techniques that served the samurai in the fifteenth and sixteenth century are much the same as those that help the freelancer win his battles in the late twentieth century.

THE ZEN OF WORKING FOR YOURSELF: PRACTICE, PATIENCE, AND PACING

Practice

How do you develop the sense of purpose and confidence that makes you a master of anything? The answer is *practice*. The great samurai may have been born with an abundance of fighting talent, but you can be sure that he put in thousands of hours of practice before achieving a high level of mastery. At one time that virtuoso was a novice who needed to conquer the most basic exercises. For hours he practiced those techniques over and over again until they became second nature; then he added new techniques, which he practiced with the same consistency and diligence. Finally, after years of practice and experience, he became a true master.

The habits that nurture successful self-employment may not require the same kind of specialized talent, but they do require a similar kind of diligence and practice if you are to become good at them. We often come across people in our seminars who say things like: "I'm a really good artist but a poor negotiator." We simply ask them how much practice and dedication has gone into their art and how much has gone into their negotiating skills. Invariably, the answer is something like: "I've spent years studying and perfecting my art, but I've never really tried to get my negotiating techniques together." Clearly, one key to mastery lies in the willingness to learn appropriate techniques and practice them over and over again.

Patience

If you've ever tried to learn a new skill, you are probably familiar with a paradox of the human condition captured in the following statement: *God give me patience and I want it now.* The understanding that meaningful accomplishments do not happen overnight is in sharp contrast to the emphasis in our fast-paced world on the "quick fix." If only you could become a phenomenal linguist in ten minutes, or write a best-selling song on your first try, or make your business the giant of its industry in a week. Many of us entertain such fantasies. After all, who wants to work hard if they don't have to?

Reconciling the need for immediate results with the reality that worthwhile achievements come about only after we complete the necessary steps is important if we intend to become successful. Did you ever take up a new sport, such as tennis? Before that first session on the court, you might have pictured a world-class player and fantasized yourself performing with a similar grace and expertise. Within the first two minutes, however, you realized that it was going to take months for you to become adequate, much less great. Greatness in all human endeavor requires mastering plateaus along the way, and that takes time!

However, there are instances of people who "caught a break," circumvented the usual steps and became instant success stories. These highly visible rarities are the grist of our fantasy mill.

Once, a young, inexperienced samurai encountered a far superior opponent who was having a bad day. A duel ensued, and much to the surprise of the young samurai, he slayed his more accomplished rival. Suddenly, the young man was reputed to possess a level of skill he could not yet even approach. Now he was expected to do battle with warriors who were far better than himself. Hardly feeling elated over his improved standing, the young samurai rightly believed that his apparent stroke of luck could well be his downfall.

No matter what business you're in the higher your standing, the more that is expected of you and the tougher the competition. Most people at the top of any field are a lot like the best swordsmen. They reached that lofty plateau only after years of preparation and many battles.

Pacing

Did you ever have the opportunity to watch a great boxer like Muhammad Ali take an opponent apart? While Ali took his time, sized up his rival, and waited for the right moment to strike, his protagonist would punch himself out and become exhausted very quickly. *Pacing* is one of the things that made Ali a great boxer. It is also an attribute that people in any field need to become great at what they do. We've seen far too many freelancers exhaust themselves with an initial burst of energy, become frustrated, and fail to reach their goals.

No matter how badly you want something to happen, you are probably not going to be able to move any mountains in the next five minutes. It is vital to understand that there are going to be many rounds in your career. Punching yourself out in the early going is counterproductive to achieving your goals. In the mad rush for instant results, we often overlook the kind of well-paced approach that underlies success in anything we attempt.

THREE VITAL HABITS FOR SUCCESSFUL SELF-EMPLOYMENT

1.   Concentration

> To be able to concentrate on the same matter
> for a considerable time is essential for difficult
> achievement.
> Bertrand Russell

Concentration is the key to living effectively in the present. People are sometimes consumed with remorse about the past and anxiety about the future. A precept not only of success, but also of emotional health is the ability to make the most out of every moment. It is easy to get sidetracked dwelling on things you have no control over, but never lose sight of the control you do

155

have over the present. The road to success and happiness begins with your ability to concentrate your energies on the here and now. With practice, distracting thoughts and feelings (about the past and future) recede as you become more able to dedicate yourself to the moment at hand.

Did you ever wake up in the morning and dive head first into an important project only to find that you were distracted not by external annoyances, but by your own thoughts? Suddenly what started out to be the matter at hand faded into the background as an endless array of thoughts fought for your attention: That muscle you pulled while you were jogging is starting to hurt. . . . Your brother is coming into town next week and you haven't

TEN THINGS TO DO WHEN YOUR CONCENTRATION GETS FUZZY

- Sit quietly, let thoughts come and go, don't follow them.

- Write out the things that are confusing you.

- Ask what the best use of your time is at this moment.

- Recheck your plan to see what else you can be doing to move toward your goal.

- Take a break.

- Go for a walk.

- Exercise.

- Call a friend.

- Your choice.

- Then come back to the matter at hand.

even made any plans yet. . . . That $500 check for completed work is long overdue, and so are your monthly bills. Two hours have gone by and your lack of concentration has prevented you from getting anything done. It's almost as though there are hundreds of tiny little demons at work conspiring to distract you.

You can improve your concentration by simply allowing the distracting thoughts to pass and then returning your attention to the matter at hand. Self-employed people often comment that the freedom of their lifestyle seems to undermine their ability to concentrate. "If I had a boss standing over me," the story goes, "I'd have no trouble concentrating. But when I work alone, my mind just seems to go off in a thousand different directions." The technique of concentration requires the discipline to ward off the forces that are pulling you away from what you are doing. Concentration helps you complete what you start with maximum energy and minimum waste of time. But how do you get through those times when you feel like you just can't maintain concentration? (see box on page 156).

2.   Staying on Course

Did you ever know somebody who could concentrate fully on whatever they were doing but who changed the focus of their energies every other week? We understand that self-employed people often prefer to juggle several careers at the same time, but when someone is forever changing the direction of their career, the flower of success never gets a chance to fully blossom. Whether you're talking to a black belt in one of the martial arts, an accomplished sculptor, or the president of a major corporation, you'll find that people who reach their goals approach what they are doing with a sense of dedication and an appreciation for continuity. It takes time to become good at anything worthwhile, so you must not only learn to concentrate, but also to maintain the focus of that concentration for extended periods of time.

In order to make sure that you are on the right course, it is important to periodically review your goals. You may need to alter your strategy along the way or even change the direction of your career entirely. But if you were writing the Great American Novel last month, composing the Great American Symphony this month, and find yourself considering a career as a financial consultant next month, it probably would be fair to say that you are not staying on course long enough to achieve success in any of these fields.

3. Stretching Yourself

Of all the techniques that nurture growth and positive change, none is more fundamental than the ability to act in the face of external obstacles and your own internal resistance. Your willingness to face challenging situations is a vital precept of growth. Meeting obstacles head on, however, is not always a pleasant experience, and there is a great temptation to back off into familiar comfort zones—"places where you feel most comfortable."[3] Such emotional retreats do provide a measure of safety and a familiar place to hide. But if we are to expand our present limits and move ahead in our lives, it is essential that we try things we've never tried and do things we've never done before. In recent years, a number of organizations have sponsored weeks in the wilderness, which include living under Spartan conditions and undertaking a number of rigorous and sometimes dangerous feats—such as swinging on a rope from one mountaintop to another. The sole purpose of such adventures is for people to stretch their internal boundaries so that they can better meet the challenges of daily living.

If you are the kind of person who tends to back away from challenging situations, you can change this habit by first recognizing your behavior and then slowly moving out of familiar comfort zones. One technique for stretching yourself involves overcoming feelings of physical and emotional discomfort. For example, did you ever sit down to work and suddenly find that you were feeling kind of down in the dumps? If you use that feeling as an excuse to go back to bed, or to suspend work and watch the tube for the remainder of the afternoon, you are retreating into a comfort zone, and maintaining the status quo.

The next time you feel that way, make yourself sit down and face the task at hand. You'll soon find those feelings of tiredness will disappear and you'll have taken a small but positive step in your growth. Every time you overcome your initial resistance to make a positive choice, you reinforce that habit and stretch yourself as a person. Each of these actions may not seem particularly significant within themselves, but cumulatively, they make a critical difference in your life. Psychologist Abraham Maslow has noted that people who generally make choices based on courage and growth rather than resistance and fear "guarantee better life choices" in general:

A person who [chooses positively] . . . each time the choice point comes will find that they add up to better choices about what is constitutionally right for him. He comes to know what his destiny is . . . [and] what his mission in life will be.[4]

SAY GOOD-BYE TO THOSE SELF-DEFEATING HABITS

AS YOU UTILIZE THE TECHNIQUES OF *CONCENTRA-tion*, *staying on course*, and *stretching yourself* to build more positive habits, you will be replacing the old habits that have been holding you back. Here are some of the self-defeating habits that inflict themselves on freelancers and some tips on how to eliminate them.

Procrastination

There's an old song called "Mañana" ("Tomorrow" in Spanish). The words go something like this: "Mañana, mañana, mañana is good enough for me." Sorry, friends, the truth is that tomorrow just doesn't cut it. If procrastination is delaying when definitive action is required, then the only ticket is to take the appropriate action. Remember, the key to making your habits work for you is to make the most of the present moment. From our point of view, there really is no such thing as procrastination, since at a given moment you are either taking action or you are not. As you learn to live in the here and now, you automatically deal with things as they come up and put procrastination off till mañana.

Thorn in the Thumb

It's amazing that the very same people who claim they can't concentrate on their work have a remarkable ability to concentrate on what's bothering them for long periods of time. Obsessing over one small area of your life to the extent that it severely hinders your ability to get things done is what we refer to as "thorn in the thumb." If you've ever had any kind of splinter, you know what we're talking about. The rest of your body feels great but that tiny area of pain has suddenly become the major factor in your life.

As Gilda Radner's hilarious character on the old "Saturday Night Live" TV show, Rosanne Rosannadanna used to say, "It's always something." If you're not waiting for the check that's supposed to be in the mail, then you're upset because your proposal might get turned down. If your proposal gets accepted, then you're worried about your dentist appointment next Monday.

If you're looking to find excuses for not taking positive action, there is indeed "always something." There are so many aspects to all of our lives, so many ways the rug can be pulled out from under our feet at any moment, we can always find that one painful area, that thorn in the thumb that keeps us from doing what we're supposed to do. The way to overcome the tendency to obsess over that one little thorn in the thumb is to pull your concentration away from the thorn and focus on all that is right in your life. There you will find many reasons to move ahead. Even during those periods when there seem to be lots of nagging little problems holding you back, you can always find some positive areas for movement. Remember: You can always find a hundred reasons not to do something, but all you need to move ahead is one good reason.

Canticide (Can't-decide)

This self-defeating habit has emerged as one of the prime killers of freelance careers in the twentieth century. There are all kinds of decisions to be made every day about any number of things. If you start thinking about them all at the same time, you're bound to become overwhelmed and unable to take action. Some people get so anxious about making decisions that it becomes virtually impossible to get anything done. This in itself is a decision not to decide, or "canticide."

The nature of most independent work requires the ability to work without supervision on projects that may not be due for months. Thus it is often tempting to indulge in thoughts like: "Maybe I don't really need to work on this today," or "What's going to happen to my career if the project doesn't turn out right?" When you are working on something that is due the next day, you are a lot like a farmer who must plant and harvest his crops when the time is right. There's no room for "canticide" in his work. Successful freelancers work harder when a deadline is near, but they also understand the importance of chipping away at a little bit of the mountain each day. Most projects require an ongoing and consistent investment of energy before they produce tangible results, so you can't allow yourself too much time wallowing in "canticide."

OVERCOMING RESISTANCE

Change requires courage and determination. It
holds the threat as well as the thrill of the unknown.
Dru Scott[5]

"Resistance represents an all-out attempt to maintain the status quo," says psychoanalyst Enid Ain. Many of us have become so accustomed to our old habits that we resist change with all the power we can muster, even when it is clear that we must change in order to progress.

Recently, a freelance architect named Mike complained that he always got paid too little for his work because he was reticent to bring up money when he took on work. Clients sensed his hesitation and wound up paying Mike far less than the standard price for his work. "I just can't seem to ask for money, and it's really starting to affect my lifestyle," he confided. We pointed out that the solution to his dilemma was simply to find a way to bring pricing into his discussion with clients at some point in the initial conversation. We helped him write out a script, which he practiced in front of the mirror and with his friends. Mike immediately began using the rehearsed statement with clients. "I was nervous about it at first," he reported, "and I'm still not particularly comfortable discussing pricing, but I can feel myself getting better at it with time and practice. And, I'm already getting better prices for my work."

Mike made a good choice by deciding to change his habit for one that was more in line with his goals. He did not say, as people often do, "this is the way I am. I just can't talk about money with my clients." Instead, he understood his habit as a behavior that could be improved without any negative consequences. Sure, he felt somewhat anxious at the beginning, but he made up his mind to grit his teeth and push through in order to get the results he was after. Why is it, though, that some people summarily resist changing their self-defeating habits? There have been various theories to explain this dynamic. Dr. Martha Friedman believes that resistance is based on people's adherence to their negative voices that mirror feelings of low self-esteem. These and other internal voices tell people they don't deserve success for the following reasons:

● My father never had it.

● My brothers and sisters never had it.

● I didn't work hard enough for it.

● I don't have the credentials.

● I'm not smart enough.

Other negative voices that underlie resistance seem to be warning people that something bad will happen to them if they become successful. These include:

● My friends won't like me.

● I won't like myself.

● I won't be able to handle the pressures.

● I will lose my creativity.

When you resist positive change because of low self-esteem, you fall into a kind of Catch-22 situation that goes something like this: If you don't like yourself, you won't take positive steps toward growth, and when you fail to take these positive steps, you like yourself even less.

Conversely, there is another kind of path that can turn the negative voices that move you back into positive ones that move you ahead. Here's how it goes:

○ Write down and recite all the reasons why you deserve to be as happy and successful as you possibly can.

○ Pay attention to these positive voices.

○ As much as possible, make positive growth choices every day.

○ Utilize the techniques for living in the present (i.e., *concentration, staying on course,* and *stretching yourself*) to solidify productive habits.

○ Acknowledge and reward yourself for your progress and use that as the basis for further growth.

Listening to your positive—rather than your negative—voices is simply another habit you can acquire by utilizing the techniques we have been discussing. Remember, you are just as deserving of success and happiness as any other human being. Also, you don't have to worry that by becoming more successful you will have to give up some other desirable aspect of your life. It is unlikely that you'll lose your creative spark if you become better at business or that your real friends will like you any less. Instead of thinking about what you might lose by changing, concentrate instead on all that you have to gain.

WHAT WOULD I GAIN BY CHANGING MY NONSERVING HABITS?

○ More time for myself

○ Greater movement toward my goals

○ Less anxiety

○ A sense of direction

○ More money

○ Less time wasted

○ Other

REACHING YOUR DESTINATION ON THE ROAD TO SUCCESS

We first make our habits—then our habits make us.
John Dryden

We believe that the journey is more important than the final destination. In contrast, we live in what a popular TV ad calls an "I want it now, get it done yesterday" world. As you explore the relevant issues and utilize the principles we have set forth, you will come up with your own answers and develop the habit of success. Your victories may seem modest at first, but as you learn to experience success, you hasten your progress and increase both the internal and external rewards that come your way.

THE ROAD TO SUCCESS: A SUMMARY

▷ Formulation of goals

▷ Development of a personal concept of success

▷ Identification of productive habits

▷ Identification of nonproductive habits

▷ Developing techniques for living in the present

▷ Overcoming resistance

▷ Replacing self-defeating habits with ones that nurture growth

166

◊ Increasing self-esteem by accumulating positive life choices

◊ Achieving goals

◊ Developing the habit of success

◊ Becoming all you are capable of

6

TIME:
Making the
Best Use of
Life's Currency

Time is the one truly irretrievable commodity in our lives. Fortunes can be lost and made again. Lovers, friends, career opportunities—and just about anything else—may reappear at some point; but time is unique. Once a day, or even an hour, is lost, it is gone forever. What you make of your time is the one major overriding consideration, not only in your work but in every aspect of your life. Those who appreciate the preciousness of every moment tend to use time well, whether they are working or playing. People who understand the finite nature of time live in the present and have a healthy perspective on the past and the future.

Learn from the Past, Don't Dwell on It

If experience is the greatest teacher, it is essential that we take from it those things that serve us well. There's a saying that goes something like this: "If a dog bites you once, it's the dog's fault; but if the same dog bites you again, it's your fault." This is just another way of saying that we must be certain to learn from our mistakes. On the other hand, it is fruitless to use those failures of the past as excuses for not making the most out of our lives right now. In order to move ahead, we must take what valuable lessons the past has to offer and turn away from the reflections of its shadows.

Aim Toward the Future; Don't Worry About It

To the extent that you are spending your time working toward goals, you are future oriented. Still, even if you are only on the first step of a five-year goal, it is important to acknowledge what you are doing *now* as being valuable for its own sake, not just as a mere rehearsal for the future. Are you getting the most value out of your time *right now* or do you feel that so much is riding on the success or failure of each project that you can't concentrate fully on the task at hand? For better or worse, it is part of the human condition that we cannot predict the future. We do, however, have a great deal of influence over the present.

Live in the Present

In order to reach your full potential, it is essential to make the matter at hand the focal point of your awareness. This involves what psychologist Abraham Maslow calls a "narrowing of consciousness": All other considerations—regrets, fears, hopes, obligations, opinions of others, etc.—must recede into the background if you are to develop the freedom and flexibility to become totally involved in the present. Here's how Maslow explains this phenomenon:

> We . . . become much less conscious of everything other than the matter in hand. . . . Insofar as [distracting] influences have affected our behavior, they no longer do so. . . . This means dropping masks, dropping our efforts to . . . please, to be lovable, to win applause. It could be said . . . [that] if we have no audience to play to, we cease to be actors. With no need to act, we can devote ourselves self-forgetfully to the problem [at hand].[1]

Time and the Empty Canvas—You Are the Artist

Whether you work as a computer software consultant, a freelance magazine writer, or a self-employed caterer, you are an artist when it comes to utilizing time. The question is: How good a time artist are you? If you think of time

171

as an empty canvas upon which you create your days, you come to realize that you can turn that canvas into a masterpiece or a mess. Do you plan big chunks of your time and fill them in with appropriate details and shadings, or do you stand in front of the big empty canvas each day and just start slopping the brush around randomly? If you think of every action you take as a single brushstroke, you come to realize that each day, week, year, and ultimately, your entire life, reflects how good a time artist you are.

Once you start looking at the time from the vantage point of *the empty canvas*, your days take on a whole new perspective. You come to realize that there are many kinds of brushstrokes you can execute upon that canvas. There are lots of little corners you can choose to work on, many colors to select from, and entire areas you might decide to use as spaces. Perhaps the two most important principles that spring from the empty canvas analogy are the way you plan your painting and the notion that no part of the canvas be thought of as wasted space. To be a good time artist, you must have an idea of what goes where on the canvas and what the total picture will look like upon completion.

How Good a Time Artist Are You?

The first step in making better use of your time is taking an honest look at how you have been handling it up until now. The following questions serve as a personal survey of how effectively you manage time. We will discuss the specific areas these questions relate to in the balance of this chapter.

1. In general, do you view considerations of time to be a big pain?

2. Do you feel you will have time to accomplish everything that is important to you?

3. Do you feel "immortal" and so there really is no hurry to get anything done?

4. Do you often feel rushed?

5. Do you feel that everything you try to do takes forever or, at the very least, ten times longer than you think it'll take?

6. Do you frequently put things off?

7. Does your use of time reflect your definition of success? (See pages 144–145.)

8. Do you establish routines to help you utilize time better, or don't you bother because you feel they are boring?

9. Do you use lists and calendars to keep track of your time, or do you keep everything in your head?

10. Can you stick to a task once you've committed a certain amount of time to it?

11. Do you lose your concentration after only a few minutes of working on anything?

12. What kinds of things tend to pull you off course?

13. What steps do you take to try to get back on course?

14. Do you know what you are supposed to be doing right now?

15. Do you often seem to get bogged down in trivial details?

16. Do you tend to dwell on the mistakes of the past?

17. Do you frequently allow fear and doubt to distract you?

18. Are you apprehensive about the future to the extent that it affects your work?

19. In general, would you say that the way you use time is a positive force in helping you achieve your goals?

Knowing What You Want— The First Step in Using Time Effectively

One of the reasons so many people are poor time artists is that they are not clear about how they want to use their time. Time consultant Angelo Valenti finds that even those who are always busy do not necessarily utilize time well:

"I find that many people are not clear about what arena they want to work in and what contribution they want to make. Consequently, they are very busy doing things that are not moving them forward. . . . You might have thirty things on a to-do list, but only four of them have the potential to make your use of time that day effective. It's not important to do more within a particular time span. It's more about how to do the right things with your time. . . . Many self-employed people are busy doing unnecessary things. They would be a lot better off and waste a lot less time if they first took a careful look at what really needs to get done."

All of this harks back to defining success for yourself and breaking down your goals (see pages 33–35). But what if you've gone through those steps and find that you still have problems managing your time?

Marge Baxter, who gives seminars on effective time use at New York University, believes that the first step is accepting that you are responsible for controlling your time:

"I start my seminars by asking people who they blame their bad time management on? People are incredibly creative when it comes to shifting the blame for why they didn't accomplish what they set out to do. They say everything from 'I didn't have the time,' or, 'I didn't have the money,' down to 'I had to stand in line at the bank.' People will do anything to avoid taking responsibility. They will blame their parents, their children, their friends, the cat, and anything else that might force them off course.

"I visualize responsibility, choice, and control as parts of a triangle. You can really raise someone's anxiety level by telling them that they are responsible for not getting that project done, or not finishing what they started. Getting people to say *I am responsible* is the first step. Because if you're not, then who is?"

The Importance of Control

The issues of responsibility and control are important for effective time use in general, but they have particular impact on men and women who work for themselves. Since self-employed people usually work on their own, they need to develop the control to follow through their plans without being supervised and told how and when to work. One of the things that undermines this kind of control is the low value some people place on their time. Here's how psychologist Martha Friedman explains this dynamic:

"Many people who work for themselves just don't consider their time valuable. Even though there are goals they want to accomplish in their business, they feel that most of their time is free time. . . . They either waste time or do unimportant things they would never bother with if they were working for a boss. What that is saying in effect is: 'What I'm doing can always be put on hold or shunted aside. I can get to it some other time.' People with that kind of mentality are going to have problems being successfully self-employed."

Keep in mind that control is not something people are born with. Like many of the other skills for successful freelancing, control can be improved by understanding its value and applying proven techniques that have helped others become better time artists.

Motivation and Reward

Okay. It's a brand new morning and here you are again standing in front of the empty canvas of your day. You have a pretty good idea of what you'd like to paint, but somehow that's not enough. You seem to get tired or distracted easily. . . . You'd like to finish your work, but there are so many things to do that you can't muster up the energy to see them all through. What to do?

A first step might be to ask yourself why you're doing what you're doing. Is it for money? Personal satisfaction? Do you feel it's something you *should* be doing for some unspecified reason? Setting your goals is very important. But without some meaningful incentive, it can be difficult to keep pushing ahead. This becomes a particular problem with long-term goals that are not likely to produce results for many months, or even years. That's why time expert Marge Baxter suggests that rewards be set up and defined before you start pursuing a goal:

"The reason we often fail to achieve our goals is that we don't ask ourselves what the reward is going to be for all our hard work. Is the reward of simply doing the task going to be enough? If not, you need to ask what else you're going to get for your effort. The reward for a major goal five years down the road is not good enough. You need some kind of built-in gratifier every time you reach a smaller plateau.

"*Motivation and reward are two sides of the same coin in that you are motivated by the things that reward you.* Our motivators are different. If you are motivated by power, you will go into a power-oriented field and your reward will be getting elected president or chairman of the board. If you don't think of goals in terms of some kind of a reward system, you are going to have problems devoting the time to achieving those goals."

Have you carefully considered what the prime motivations in your career are? Here are seven of the most frequently mentioned incentives that inspire freelancers to use their time well. Take a few minutes to consider which are most important to you:

☞   **Staying in business**

☞   **Earning more money**

☞   **Living the lifestyle you choose**

☞   **Personal satisfaction**

☞   **Recognition of peers**

☞ Becoming the best in your field

☞ Making a significant contribution to your field and/or to mankind

Since rewards and motivation go hand in hand, look over your goals and make sure for each plateau you've built in a reward to acknowledge your progress. Here are some rewards that people often give themselves. Add your own to the list.

☞ Taking a vacation

☞ Going out in style

☞ Giving yourself an extra day for pleasure

☞ Spending money on an extravagance

☞ Doing nothing

One particular problem that self-employed people have in the area of motivation and reward is aligning their business and personal goals. Freelancers—particularly in the arts—often do one kind of work for money and another for inner gratification. Without a sense that these activities feed into one another, there is often confusion and a vague obstacle to movement in both areas. There are a variety of ways to resolve these difficulties, depending on the specific situation. Let's take a case in point.

Laura earns a good living as a freelance advertising copywriter, whereas her real passion in life is writing musical theater. When she first came to see us, she felt torn apart by what she viewed as two disparate areas of her life. She told us:

"I'm having problems being productive in both things. I need the money that copywriting brings in, and I have this longing to do musical theater full time. Unfortunately, there is no way to make any money doing musicals unless you have a hit play, and that's not likely to happen any time soon. What's going on is this: Whenever I'm supposed to be working on a copywriting assignment, I daydream about doing the thing I really love; and when I'm working on musical theater, I get depressed because I'm afraid that nothing tangible is ever going to come of it."

Laura now understands the situation in a different light. She realizes that her money-making assignments do have the potential to feed into her passion. We suggested that she put a percentage of her earnings aside for the specific purpose of investing it in rehearsal space, fees for musicians and actors, and other expenses involved in showcasing her musical theater projects.

Aligning her business and personal goals has helped Laura apportion and utilize her time much more effectively. "I'm starting to get much more of a sense that the different areas of my life fit together," she reports. "Now that I can look at it this way, I'm able to put much more of myself into both aspects of my work." In essence, Laura has set up a system in which the money she makes from her copywriting rewards her by allowing her to put more resources into her dream. Conversely, the progress that she is making in her musical theater work has become a strong motivation to make more money as a copywriter.

Priorities: First Things First

One of the most interesting things we have noticed about freelancers after they become aware of the value of time is that they go from saying things like "God, I just don't know what

I'm going to do today," to "There's so much to get done, I've got no idea how I'll ever get to all of it." Successful freelancers are aware of how little time there is in a day to do all the things that are screaming to be taken care of. That's why it's essential to spend the most time working on things that have the greatest value.

How do you go about figuring out which things merit your precious time? Should you spend more time completing assignments or should you be out there hustling up new clients? Should you be more concerned with paying the rent or with fulfilling your dreams? Obviously, all these things deserve some of your time, but which are most important? Time expert Marge Baxter finds that freelancers are often unclear about their priorities.

"The real issue for people who work for themselves is recognizing what is most important. The bulk of your time should be spent on things that justify your having a particular goal. . . . I know writers, for example, who will tell you they went to the bank and the post office, did the dishes, or whatever. But if you ask them if they wrote anything today or called to set up an appointment with a potential client, they say, 'I just didn't get around to it.'"

If you want to spend more of your time on priorities, you can start by taking the following steps:

1. Set goals in each major area of your life (work, personal, family, and health) that coincide with your definition of success (see pages 125–126).

2. Select the one goal in each area that is most important. These are your priorities.

3. Construct a schedule that devotes the most time to the highest-priority goals.

4. Schedule priorities during times when you work best.

Prime Time: When You Work Best

We all have different times of the day when we're at our best, or at least at our best in relation to certain tasks. If, for example, you are a writer and know you do your best writing in the morning, make sure you don't use that time to go to the post office. Most creative activities require a good deal of energy and concentration. People tend to accomplish more in less time if they work on these activities when they are at their best.

One of the major advantages of working for yourself is that, to a great extent, you can do what you want when it suits you. Yet most people don't even begin to take advantage of this opportunity to work on priorities at their best times. Imagine if you worked nine-to-five and had to do particular tasks in accordance with company policy. Say you were employed as a public relations account executive, and you did your best writing in the morning. Despite your preferences, your employer scheduled meetings four mornings a week, thus relegating all writing to the afternoon hours. People with nine-to-five jobs come up against situations like this all the time.

When you are self-employed, you have a lot more flexibility in matching your prime-time hours with your priorities. This matching process is essential for getting more quality work accomplished in less time. However, many freelancers remain unaware of their most productive times even after they figure out their priorities. People go through a lot of agony and frustration that could be avoided by simply scheduling tasks at more appropriate times.

You can't put square pegs in round holes

When you were younger, did you ever take that test where you were asked to match different shaped pegs and holes? No matter how hard you tried, it was impossible to jam a square peg into a round hole. The same principle applies when you try to match different activities with the most appropriate times to work on them. It is essential to figure out what times of the day you can best accomplish your priorities, and schedule those things first. Here are some suggestions to help you put the square pegs in the square holes and the round pegs in the round holes:

1. Make a note of when you seem to have the most energy for different activities and try to reflect this in your schedule.

2. As much as possible, schedule priorities during periods of highest energy.

3. When you feel frustrated because you can't concentrate on what you are doing, switch to an alternate priority activity.

4. Protect high-energy periods by eliminating all distractions.

5. At low energy times do less demanding work—such as filing, errands, organizing, writing letters.

CREATING THE LIFESTYLE YOU WANT

Outside Influences

No matter how much freedom your lifestyle affords you, clients, your family, and the rest of the planet have their own constraints which may not totally coincide with yours. For example, an important client may only be reachable in the morning during hours when you may be relatively uncommunicative and much better at doing creative work. There are also the pressures of deadlines that can cause you to work around the clock. Finally, all freelancers are subject to unexpected occurrences— welcome or unwelcome—that can screw up their schedules if they aren't flexible enough to deal with them. People who work alone may feel fortunate to have interactions with the outside world, even if sometimes they are disruptive. The trick is to keep experimenting until you come up with a schedule that allows you both to accomplish your goals for the day and to accommodate the unexpected.

Night People Versus Day People

One of the most talked-about issues in certain fields is the benefits of working nights as opposed to days. Some kinds of work are by their very nature nightwork, and there's simply no

Some jobs require late hours.

getting around it. If you're a nightclub musician, you work day ends at 2:00 or 3:00 A.M., and this tends to turn you into a night person—no matter what your preference. On the other hand, some people would *rather* work through the night and sleep away a good part of the day. Theoretically, there should be no difference between someone who works from 8:00 A.M. to 5:00 P.M., and the one who works from 9:00 P.M. to 5:00 A.M. However, there is something to be said for conducting your business during hours that are at least somewhat compatible with the rest of the world. For one thing, it is often impossible to reach people in their offices except during standard business hours. Also, many freelancers report that they feel less isolated not only from the business community at large, but also from their family and friends, if they pattern their work day to coincide with those of the relevant people in their lives.

Considerations That Can Affect Your Use of Prime Time

★ Coordinating with the nine-to-five world

★ Coordinating with other freelancers you work with

★ Coordinating with your family and friends

★ Finding common synch points with the rest of the world may involve some adjustments in your use of time, such as:

    ☆ getting up earlier

    ☆ rescheduling key activities

    ☆ persuading others to adapt to your lifestyle.

Handling Multiple Projects

One of the keys for freelancers who want to make the most of their time is understanding how to deal with multiple projects. There is something to be said for concentrating all your energies on one primary goal, as P. T. Barnum points out in *How to Become a Money Getter*:

> Engage in one kind of business only and stick to it faithfully until you succeed or until your experience shows that you should abandon it. Hammering on one nail will generally drive it home. . . . When a man's undivided attention is centered on one object, his mind will constantly be suggesting improvements of value which would escape him if his brain was occupied by a dozen different subjects at once.[2]

For better or worse, many freelancers find it either necessary or desirable to be involved with several projects at the same time. Some have multiple goals that they are trying to fulfill. Phyllis, for example, is an architectural consultant who earns an average of $25,000 a year. Though she likes her work well enough, her real passion is painting large abstract works of art. Because she has never made any money from her passion and doesn't want to compromise her comfortable lifestyle, she paints during the evening hours, after putting in a full day working on paying projects.

"I wish I could make enough money doing what I love most," Phyllis told us recently. "But I understand that for me right now this is an ideal situation. I consider myself lucky because I'm able to earn pretty good money doing something I like and still have enough time and energy left over to pursue my dream."

From our point of view, Phyllis is doing a good job juggling her multiple goals. She understands the role each one plays in her total scheme. By pinpointing the best times to concentrate on both goals, she manages to put forth enough effort to move forward in her work and her passion. Unfortunately, other freelancers we see have all kinds of difficulties handling multiple projects.

With all respect to P. T. Barnum, there are a number of good reasons to be involved with more than one project. Freelancers, particularly at the start of their careers, may need to exercise several of their talents and skills in order to determine which will allow them to stay afloat as viable self-employed business people. Even more experienced freelancers sometimes have to accept several projects in one or more areas of work in order to pay the rent. This is especially true if you are in a seasonal business when all the work comes in at the same time. In an ideal world, you would ply your trade in only one major area and put all your attention into a single job. But, alas, we live in a world that is not quite ideal. One of the realities most of us have to deal with is the necessity of juggling several things at the same time.

Multiple project syndrome (MPS)

Let's pretend that you are currently involved with three projects. One of these is bringing in the major portion of your income for the month; another is a low-paying, overdue project you took several months ago because nothing else was coming in at the time; and a third—which generates no money at all—relates to your passion. Any one of these projects could occupy your mind fully. You could, for example, become obsessed with your non-paying passion and totally neglect the work that is paying the rent; or, you could become depressed over your inability to complete the overdue project, and sit around and do nothing for days on end.

Once you've committed to take on a project, you pretty much have to do it. The one thing to avoid at all costs is thinking about the total amount of work required for all three projects at the same time, and becoming so overwhelmed that you wind up doing no work at all. We call this "Multiple Project Syndrome" (MPS).

Here is a brief summary of how the principles of effective time use apply to the handling of projects to which you've already committed:

- Consider each project in terms of the goals it is moving you toward.

- Determine what step you are currently up to on each project and work only on that.

- Review your motivation for working on the project in the first place.

- Make sure there are rewards for each plateau you complete.

- Determine which of these projects are priorities.

- Schedule your work on each project during appropriate times for you.

- When working on a project, ask yourself: What is the best use of my time right now?

- Don't become overwhelmed by MPS: Avoid thinking about the big picture.

In order to avoid getting done in by Multiple Project Syndrome in the future, it is essential to evaluate each project that comes your way *before* taking it on. Freelancers, especially during the early stages of their careers, feel obligated to take any paying project that comes their way. Money is always seductive, but often the dollars involved relative to the time spent on a project add up to a bad deal. A young trumpet player named Jim, who also drives a cab to make ends meet, learned to avoid MPS by turning down projects that didn't make sense for him:

"When I first got out of school, I was so anxious to get my career rolling that I automatically accepted any job that came my way. This became a problem in that many of the jobs paid poorly and didn't really benefit me in any other way. I've got a different way of looking at it now. Unless a job puts me in contact with relevant people in my field, expands my horizons as a musician, pays me substantial money, or does something else that moves me ahead in my career, I turn it down. Believe me, driving a taxi is something I hope to get out of as soon as possible. But at least it's helping me pay the rent and make more intelligent decisions about what work I take."

Accepting New Projects

In an economy where there is a scarcity of work in so many fields, it is often difficult to turn down paying projects. Still, taking a job just because somebody offers it to you can ultimately be a very bad business decision. One reason free-lancers sometimes give for taking a project is: "What else could I do? It was the only offer I had." In our experience, we have rarely encountered a situation where a person has absolutely no alternative. Sometimes the choice comes down to turning a job down and working part time as a waiter or taxi driver. In other instances, it may become necessary to leave freelancing for awhile and take a full-time job. The point is: There usually is a choice and that choice is yours.

When you are offered a project in any field, there is no definite way of knowing where it will lead you, especially if it is a type of project you have never worked on before. There are all kinds of stories—particularly in show business—of people who turned down a job that led to fame and fortune for the person who accepted it. More often than not, though, people who turn an offer down because they have a gut feeling that it is wrong for them generally have no regrets. Also, don't fall for the line that a project will be fast and easy to complete. Freelancers in all fields report that jobs tend to take more—not less—time than they originally anticipated. As one graphic designer friend likes to say: "Everything is quicksand," by which he means that any project you get started on tends to suck up lots of your precious time, *especially* when someone tells you that it will hardly take any time at all. Learning to discriminate which projects are worth your investment in time and effort is an essential skill for successful freelancing.

Here are some important questions to ask before accepting a project in any field:

SHOULD I TAKE THE JOB?

1. What is the exact nature of the project?

2. How much time will it entail?

3. How much will it pay?

4. How much of a profit will I make?

5. What kind(s) of work will I have to do to complete the project?

6. Will I be able to delegate some of the work to others?

7. Is this a kind of job I enjoy?

8. How is this project likely to further my career?

9. Will taking on this project give me visibility with important contacts in the future?

10. What is the reputation and track record of the client who is hiring me?

11. What current projects (if any) will this take time from?

12. Does this project relate directly or indirectly to my major goals?

13. Is there any additional information I require before making my decision?

TIME FRAMEWORKS— CREATING YOUR OWN RULES

ONE OF THE THINGS NINE-TO-FIVERS LIKE TO SAY to freelancers is: "How do you make yourself put in a good day's work without anyone else telling you when you should be at work and what you should be doing while you're there?" On some level, this question can be translated as follows: "What a great life you must have being able to work when you want to. If I didn't have my boss to answer to, I'd work when I wanted and that probably wouldn't be very often. Freelancing must be like some kind of permanent vacation."

If you are serious about your career, you know that people who characterize the freelance life as this terrific kind of self-indulgence know not of what they speak. In fact, the lack of externally imposed rules and structure on their work day is one of the things people who work for themselves find most difficult. We can visualize people who work nine-to-five as participating in a game where the precedents and rules have been pretty well defined. Freelancers, on the other hand, are involved in a game where no rules have ever been spelled out. Our purpose in this chapter is to provide guidelines for managing your time, but you are going to have to create your own rules and stick to them.

If you've just started working for yourself after having been at a nine-to-five job for a period of time, you may feel quite rudderless unless you impose some rules for yourself and stick to them. Your ability to do so can, as much or more than any other single factor, determine your success. Time expert Marge Baxter strongly believes in setting up routines and following them faithfully:

"I think it's very important for freelancers to set a specific time to start work each day, get dressed, and start plugging away. . . . Writers, for example, often talk about how tough it is to face the blank page and create something that goes on it. Yet every successful writer I've come across says, 'I've got my own little room and I sit at my typewriter every day for a certain number of hours.' They have a structured routine to prevent them from saying 'I'm not into writing today.' Even if they have writer's block, they still sit behind the typewriter for those specified hours."

Anchors

Although you may decide to leave some of your time flexible, it usually helps to develop the habit of doing one or two of your most important tasks during the same time every day. This tends to take the anxiety out of trying to find a different time to concentrate on your priorities. If you're an illustrator, you want to make sure you're at the drawing table every day at your prime-time hours. You can fit less important items in the spaces that remain after you've taken care of the work that most strongly relates to your goals. Marge Baxter calls this finding "anchors" in your day:

"I think it's best to start building routines by working around two poles. If you have two activities to look forward to each day, the rest of your time will tend to fall into place. When you wake up in the morning with no idea of what you are going to do, it can cause you to fall apart. Many freelancers do well when they schedule one work and one leisure anchor for themselves. If, for example, you can work on your priorities from 9:00 A.M. till noon, and jog or play tennis from 4:00 to 5:00 P.M., you'll probably find that you'll be extremely productive."

One technique that often helps freelancers stick to their routines or anchors is committing to someone else. When you work alone, you don't have that sense of urgency that comes from knowing that someone else is depending on you to get the job done. For example, if you have a project that isn't due for three months, it might help to tell the client you'll submit part of it at the end of one month, even if this is not a requirement. Part of the problems freelancers face in coping with a lack of structure is a sense that they have too much time in relation to a particular project. Establishing deadlines for yourself by making promises to others is one way of creating your own rules.

Creating Your Day

Here are some questions that will help you arrive at a schedule that suits your specific needs:

1. How many hours a day do you need to work to achieve your goals?

2. What time would you like to be working by?

3. What time does that mean *you* have to get up (include your morning routines of exercise, reading the paper, etc.)?

4. What time would you like to be asleep by?

5. Do you like to get in a little reading before going to sleep?

6. Does having a decent breakfast help you start the day?

7. Does exercise help you start the day?

8. Do you only have coffee and a cigarette in the morning?

9. What time would you like to be finished working by?

10. Do you need time out for lunch?

11. If you like to work long stretches, what kind of short breaks could you take?

12. What time do you like to have dinner?

13. Do you eat dinner so late that it keeps you up?

14. What social time can you use to balance working alone all day (calls, meals, hanging out after work is done)?

15. When are you at your absolute worst during the day for accomplishing things that take a great deal of concentration?

16. When are you at your best?

Building in Time-Savers and Eliminating Time-Wasters

"To spend time is to utilize it in a specified manner," martial arts expert Bruce Lee once noted. "To waste time is to expend it thoughtlessly or carelessly. We all have time to either spend or waste, and it is our decision what to do with it. But once passed, it is gone forever."[3]

When you become aware of how valuable your time really is, and determine how you want to use it, there are a number of relatively simple things you can do to get the most out of every day.

Delegate low priority tasks

Imagine that you were hired as a corporate executive for $50,000 a year. Do you think you would spend time performing menial or clerical tasks that are worth, perhaps, $5 an hour? Not likely. Why is it, then, that so many freelancers complain that they are bogged down with these nonpriority activities? Marge Baxter feels that it's because they often don't really know how much their time is worth:

"Freelancers routinely spend $20 solving a $3 problem. If you ask them to put a dollar value on how much their time is worth, they often don't have an answer. This leads to almost bizarre ways of utilizing time. What, for example, is a freelancer whose time is worth $50 an hour doing typing an envelope, which is a $4-an-hour task? In some cases, they just don't want to spend the money; meanwhile, it is costing them a lot more money to do the task themselves. I say: *Buy low value time*. Hire a secretary or clerical assistant for five hours a week. The key is to pay someone substantially less than your hourly fee to do nonpriority work."

The following questions can help you decide if you are wasting time working on tasks you would be better off delegating:

■ Do you work longer hours getting your work done than most people in your field?

■ Are you swamped with paperwork and other low-priority tasks?

■ Do you spend most of your working hours concentrating on priorities?

■ Do you feel that even the smallest detail is so critical that it requires your personal attention?

■ Do you find that you have little or no time for leisure?

To determine whether or not you ought to delegate a particular task, ask yourself these questions:

- ■ Are you the only one who can do the task?

- ■ If not, who else can do it?

- ■ How much will it cost to hire someone to do the task?

- ■ How does that compare to your estimation of what an hour of your time is worth?

- ■ What priority activity will you be concentrating on if you delegate this task?

Screen out interruptions

No matter what kind of work you do, there are bound to be certain times in the day when you need a few hours of undisturbed concentration. Successful people learn to become positively territorial about these valuable chunks of *prime time:* More often than not, it pays off. Time consultant Angelo Valenti describes how one of his clients deals with this vital issue:

"Anna is now a casting director for a leading daytime TV soap opera. When she was an assistant casting director, she had a problem of constantly being interrupted by actors, directors, and production people. She needed a block of time to get her planning and scheduling done each day, and these interruptions were costing her. What she did was decide to put a note on her office door between the hours of 9:00 and 11:30 that read: '*Anna loves you but she cannot be disturbed.* Between 2:00 and

5:00 P.M., you can interrupt her all you want, but during those morning hours, she is simply not available.' The impact of this was immediate. She started getting more of the right work done in less time, and three weeks later she was promoted."

Anna's problem is familiar to those of us who have worked in an office setting. Those of us who work out of our homes have a slightly different version of the same problem. It's not so much people stopping by as problems relating to the telephone. People who work in offices tend to assume that freelancers are always available to kill some time with. "I've got a few minutes to kill," they say to themselves. "Let me call Joe and chew the fat." Let's say Joe is a freelance costume designer working diligently on an important design. Suddenly, the phone rings and he feels that he has to answer it. After all, he reasons, maybe it's a new client with a job that will turn his career around, or news of a huge inheritance from some long-lost relative. At the very least, it is

People who work at home are subject to unexpected interruptions.

some kind of contact with the outside world, both reminding and relieving him of his loneliness.

The Mystique of the Phone

The phone rings. You drop whatever you are doing, trip over furniture, and let the toast burn in your mad rush to get the phone. Your heart rate increases as you race for the sacred instrument of communication, desperately hoping to reach it before it stops ringing. (Too late—they hung up.)

Freelancers often complain about phone interruptions as though they were an insurmountable problem. When we present them with the simple alternative of employing an answering service or buying a telephone answering machine, they seem surprised that there really is something they can do to eliminate the problem. By this time, we've all dealt with services and machines and we're well aware of their disadvantages. "I hate those mechanical devices," people often complain, "and I hang up on them without leaving a message. I would never own such a machine, because I'm philosophically opposed to them and assume people would hang up on me."

We have conducted our own informal survey of how people relate to answering machines. The consensus seems to be that if the call is important enough, the caller will leave a message. If someone really needs you for a job, they are not likely to hang up on the machine. Most of the hangups come from friends calling to rap or salespeople who are cold canvassing. There are some businesses where people really do need to answer the phone personally during certain times of the day or week, but few that require twenty-four hour accessibility. We strongly recommend that you consider designating at least part of your prime time as hours when you are unavailable to callers. Here are some suggestions:

Tips for Eliminating Telephone Interruptions

☎ If your budget allows it, employ an answering service, especially one which specializes in your field. They will track you down if an important calls comes in.

☎ Answering machines are the next best thing to a real person answering the phone. You can purchase one for about $100. If you are out a lot, for a little more money, you may want a machine with a remote control feature.

☎ If you are expecting an important call during hours that you don't want to be interrupted, you can screen your calls by listening to who it is leaving the message. Most machines now include a feature that allows you to listen to a call while the caller is putting his or her message on tape and then to cut in and take the call. Some freelancers like to keep their machines on and screen calls at all times. This allows them to talk to who they want when they want.

☎ If you find that you are getting a lot of hangups, you may want to change your message. Some people go in for music in the background; others try a comic approach. We find that a short, simple, businesslike message does the job quite nicely. We also find that most hangups really weren't that important.

☎ When the phone rings and the caller says "It's important," ask yourself: "Important to whom?" If you decide that call is not important to you, then you are under no great obligation to answer it.

☎ Set an appropriate tone when answering the phone. If you left your answering machine off because you were expecting an important call, but it is a friend or someone else you don't have time to speak with, let that person know that you are glad to hear from them but that your time is limited. This approach usually helps the caller get to the real reason he called rather quickly. It is essential to let people know that you are quite busy and unavailable for meaningless interruptions during working hours.

☎ Establish your own call-back system. Select a time during which you answer all calls. If possible, make it the same time every day, and let people know that you are available at that hour.

Cut IT out (cut out Implementation Time)

Implementation Time is the length of time that goes by between when you decide to do something and when you actually do it. If you've set up an IBS for yourself, your actions in a given day come from decisions and plans that were formulated earlier. It is crucial that you get right into action without wasting any time. If you were working as an employee, your supervisor might hand you some work that he or she wants completed immediately. It would be inappropriate for you to agonize over the difficulty or unattractiveness of that particular project: Your job would be simply to do the necessary work. Freelancers sometimes have difficulty looking at their work in that light. They tend to question and reexamine every single move instead of getting down to the business at hand. Psychologist Martha Friedman finds that some freelancers will find any trivial activity to occupy their time so long as it is unrelated to their career priorities:

"If you find yourself doing a lot of chores unrelated to your main goals and you realize those chores are unimportant . . . [you are] undermining your success. One self-employed client I work with, who is very wealthy, spends a good portion of his time getting his Mercedes fixed. Other clients tell me they spend most of their days cooking or taking care of the kids. If these people were working for a boss, they wouldn't have time for that kind of stuff."

If you've set a goal for yourself and made plans to implement it, don't let doubt and anxiety cause you to abandon it for some low-priority task that provides little or no movement toward your objectives. Instead, use what time expert Alan Lakein calls the "Swiss cheese method"—poke holes in an overwhelming priority project. This is accomplished by thinking of some five-minute "instant tasks" that break the project down into manageable units. Here are some of Lakein's suggestions for making this method work:

> Make a list of possible instant tasks. . . . It doesn't really matter [which ones] you select as long as [they are]: (1) Easy—the easier the better—and (2) Related to the overwhelming [priority activity]. How much of a contribution a particular instant task will make to getting your [priority] done is far less important than the overriding objective of the moment: To do something—anything—on the [priority]. Whatever you choose, you'll at least have begun. [4]

Let's say you are working on a major project that you've estimated will take a hundred hours. The thought of that much work can be paralyzing, but there are many five-minute "instant tasks" that you can do to chip away. If you set fifteen minutes aside, you can tackle three five-minute tasks. These might include: calling up someone to arrange for an interview in the future; organizing the paperwork for the current chapter; and

Keep long-range goals in mind even when engaged in menial tasks.

making a list of tasks that can be delegated to others. Keep in mind that any one of these tasks might temporarily lead to a dead end. You may, for example, find that the person you tried to contact for an interview will be out of town for the next six months. (Such a setback, as Lakein astutely observes, might even give you a sense of relief in that it serves as an excuse for why you couldn't get anything accomplished on the project that day). The important thing at that point is to move on to a different five-minute task until you find one that gets you involved working on your goal. Let's say you start organizing your paperwork and discover a topic that holds your attention. Before you know it, you start taking notes and you've spent an hour on the task.

Breaking up major projects in this way helps avoid lengthy Implementation Time or unproductive transitions between planning and action. You may also find it useful to employ slightly longer "instant tasks" of perhaps ten or fifteen minutes. But remember, in order to really have an impact, these activities must relate to a priority goal.

Eliminate procrastination

We have spoken about procrastination as a self-defeating habit in the previous chapter. Because it is such an all-pervasive time killer, we feel it deserves further discussion in this context. There is a law of physics that maintains the following: A body at rest tends to stay at rest while a body in motion tends to stay in motion. This is the essence of procrastination. Did you ever ask yourself what causes you to avoid getting down to work: Are you overwhelmed by the sheer quantity of work that needs to get done? Frustrated because you feel your efforts won't produce results? Anxious that even if you do finish, your work won't be good enough? Time expert Marge Baxter finds that people who feel the need to be perfect are often chronic procrastinators:

> "People tend to procrastinate because they feel they can't do something well. They have the idea that it is mandatory to do things perfectly on the first try. This notion can come from your upbringing and from the kind of grading systems most of us were exposed to in school. We've all had the following trip laid on us at one time or another: If you're not perfect, something terrible is going to happen to you. The trick is to aim for excellence but not perfection."

When you reflect on things you've done in the past, ask yourself if you've tried your best. People know when they've given a project their best shot. Perfection is an unrealistic concept and a handy excuse for doing nothing at all, so try to steer clear of that kind of thinking. Instead, establish high standards for your work. If you wish, make it a goal to become the best person in your field. Just remember, perfection is, apparently, not part of the human condition: The best baseball players get a hit only one-third of the time; the greatest artists produce some turkeys; the most skilled negotiators lose once in a while; and the most renowned consultants sometimes give incorrect advice.

Another noteworthy tendency of people who procrastinate is that they cling to the hope that the task they've been delaying will magically disappear. That's why Marge Baxter calls procrastination "the high side of anxiety":

"We learn to procrastinate as very small children about things we don't want to do. Even though we feel guilty about not doing what we're supposed to, we're convinced that we'll somehow be rescued. As I tell my clients, 'There is no fairy godmother, she's gone to Hawaii. *No one can rescue you but yourself.*'"

If you want to keep procrastination from eating away your precious time, try dealing with things as they come up instead of forever putting them off. This way, you never have to devote time and energy to those tasks again. Procrastinating very often drains more of your energy than actually taking care of the problem at hand. Also, when the things you are putting off mount up sufficiently, your sense of frustration and anxiety increase as well. Try writing down the things you are procrastinating about so that you can look at them more objectively and formulate a reasonable plan of action. Take a few minutes to fill in the accompanying chart. Try to pinpoint one or more "instant tasks" that can get you moving toward your goal. Pick one and take action on it today:

THINGS I AM PROCRASTINATING ABOUT:	REASON I CAN'T GET GOING:	REWARD FOR TAKING ACTION	"INSTANT TASKS" TO HELP SOLVE A PROBLEM RIGHT NOW

Know When You're Working and When You're Not Working

Do you know what it is you're supposed to be doing right now? Are you working? If so, what are you working on, and how much time have you committed to that task? As we've noted earlier, everybody is busy doing something, the question is to what end? Richard, a freelance writer, had a problem figuring out how to best use his time. He'd often wander around his home/office, unable to really get down to work, but feeling too pressured to relax. Finally, he came to the following conclusion: "In order to make good use of time, you need to **know when you're working and when you're not working.**"

Since our friend told us of his revelation, we've been having some fun with this little parable. How easy it is, on a day when you feel like procrastinating, to say: "I'm not going to do any work today, but that's okay. At least I know I'm not working." Actually, this little joke has more than a grain of truth in it. If you know that you're simply too exhausted or distracted or whatever to get anything accomplished, perhaps it would be a good idea to take part of the day (or even the entire day) off. You might imagine that chronic procrastinators are adept at this particular aspect of time usage since they often do nothing (except procrastinate, of course). Actually, this type of person can have as hard a time relaxing as he does working. Since he feels so guilty about not getting any work done, he tends to agonize just as strenuously when he takes time off.

For those of us who spend the majority of our waking hours pursuing our goals, rest and relaxation are essential—not only to replenish our creative resources but also to feel that a portion of our time exists for our personal pleasure. This balance between work and rest time we call *Goal, no goal.* Successful people (as we define the term) aim for high-quality leisure in the same way they aim for high quality in their work. If they take an afternoon, or even an hour, off, they seek out activities that offer them something valuable. Many self-employed people jog or engage in some other physical activity several times a week; some like to take a few hours off once in a while to see a movie in the afternoon; one highly successful financial consultant gets tremendous pleasure out of going to the track; while a famous nonfiction author takes a half hour out every afternoon to watch her favorite

Know when you're working and when you're not.

television soap opera. In every case, these freelancers set aside time for a leisure activity they enjoy both for its own sake and to make it easier for them to return to their goal-oriented work.

There is another type of person, aside from the procrastinator, who has problems utilizing leisure time. This type is called a workaholic because, in a very real sense, he (or she) is addicted to work. This type of individual characteristically rushes from one task to another without any real overriding sense of direction. Leisure and rest are, of course, out of the question because there's always more work to do. Workaholics are not effective time users partly because they don't ever get sufficient rest to keep working at very high levels. The trick is to work hard enough to feel you deserve some leisure, and to consider that leisure every bit as important to your life as your work.

Take your leisure time "off the top"

You might recall that in our discussion of money, we stressed the need to take out for savings a percentage of every check that comes in. We believe that freelancers ought to take the same approach toward leisure and vacations. Don't wait until you think you have time to relax. Build leisure hours and days into your schedule now, or—like your potential savings dollars—they will slip away forever. If you are working for a company, you would need to know when your days off are, how many breaks you have every day, what holidays you are off, and how much vacation time you have coming. These are not luxuries, but necessities that allow people to enjoy life and also work more productively. As a self-employed individual, you want to make certain that periods of rest, leisure, and vacations are built into your life. Remember, these are neither time wasters nor things to be scheduled in only after everything else is in place. On the contrary, your leisure time is a significant and indispensable part of your life that ought not be neglected or shunted aside.

For best results—ORGANIZE

One of the time wasters freelancers talk about most is their lack of organization. So frequent and redundant are these complaints, they've begun to take on the ring of familiar songs. There's the "I'm inundated with paperwork" rag and the "I can't ever find things when I need them" waltz. Most dramatic of all is the "I'm a complete slob" blues. We don't mean to make light of these problems, well aware as we are of the havoc they can wreak. Most of us could use some improvement in the way we are organized. Yet this seems to be an area in which people are particularly resistant to change. We asked Maggie Cadman, president of Let's Get Organized, for some basic concepts to keep in mind when confronting this problem. She believes that the first step is to have a clear picture of what you want to organize for:

"Freelancers need to determine what they specifically want to do—keeping in mind that they can always go in lots of other directions some time in the future. The question is: What's really important today? Once you decide what the thing is—whether it's bringing in a certain amount of money or some other goal—you set up a system for it so that things don't get lost or fall through the cracks. Basically, what you are doing is eliminating everything that isn't necessary and effectively handling what's left."

Cadman's advice seems simple and logical enough. Still, she finds that many people have a kind of built-in block when it comes to getting organized. Cadman feels that—like procrastination—disorganization is due in no small measure to a misplaced notion of perfection:

"People think they must be perfect, and if they can't be perfect, they might as well go to hell in a hand basket. They really don't see that *the reason for being organized is to allow you to relax and not have to pay attention to the minor details of your life. People who are organized spend more (not less) time doing things they want to do.*"

When you think of a well-organized person, do you picture somebody who has all their things in some kind of beautiful, immaculate order? If so, you may be using that as an excuse for not getting organized. Instead of thinking of organization as the reflection of a perfectly ordered human being, try thinking of it as the creation of systems that help make life easier and enhance your success as a freelancer. We have entered the offices of self-employed people that looked as if they were hit by an earthquake. Nevertheless, the proprietors of these quarters were able to locate whatever they needed in short order, thus meeting and often exceeding Maggie Cadman's major criterion for organization, namely:

"Can you find what you are looking for in five minutes or less?"

If you can answer yes to this question, then you are reasonably well organized. Still, there is one other question you might want to ask about your system of organization, and that is: *Could someone other than you understand your system well enough to find something of importance?* If the answer is no, you might want to consider restructuring your systems so that they are understandable to others. You may not feel that such considerations are critical, but what if you were on your way to an important appointment and needed the address? Could your spouse or secretary locate your appointment book? What if you were out of town and a client called for an important document? Would someone be able to penetrate the systems you created? Actually, it might not be a bad idea to evaluate your organizational systems from the point of view of an outside consultant (not your mother!) who was called in to suggest some functional improvements. Taking that perspective, answer the following questions:

HOW WELL-ORGANIZED ARE YOU?

- Does the nature of the workspace seem to enhance the type of work this person is concentrating on?

- Are the most frequently used tools and equipment in a place where they can be easily reached?

- Is there evidence of a reasonably efficient filing system?

- Is the workspace conducive to relaxing if the person wants to take a short break?

- Is there adequate ventilation and lighting to work without strain or distraction?

- Conversely, is the space so conducive to relaxation that it might be difficult to get anything accomplished?

- Are there materials from a number of projects scattered about? (Most organizational experts recommend that materials from only one project at a time should be on your desk.)

- Does the general clutter and chaos of the workspace make it hard to focus on the matter at hand?

In answering the last two questions, keep in mind that our primary interest is in results, not beauty. Some organizational experts are automatically put off by clutter, but we can only support their view to the extent that it hinders getting work accomplished. This notion was humorously expressed by Michael LeBoeuf in *The Productivity Challenge* when he asked: "If a cluttered desk means a cluttered mind, what does an empty desk mean?"[5]

Get out from under all that paperwork

Paper, paper, paper—one of the true pains of our age. Every day it mounts up: Junk mail (how did they ever get your address in the first place?); bills—it's bad enough you have to pay them, you certainly don't need the additional paper; business correspondence; personal correspondence; thank-you notes; your welcome notes; memos; greeting cards; etc., ad nauseam. What to do with all that paper? There's an old adage that helps: *When in doubt, throw it out!* That's simple enough, isn't it? If you're staring at a piece of paper and wondering if it's worth keeping, chances are it isn't. If, as organization expert Stephanie Winston claims, paper is not supposed to be "a smoldering weight in your life . . . but a cue and a trigger for action,"[6] it makes sense to keep only those pieces of paper that have the potential of serving you in this way. In that case, you can probably eliminate 90 percent of all the paper you presently keep in your files. Here's what Maggie Cadman tells her clients about handling paper:

"The basic rule is to keep those things you originate yourself because there's no other way of replacing it except by re-creating it. It follows that if someone else creates something, they ought to keep a copy in case you need it again. I'm not saying toss things out indiscriminately. But if you think there's no immediate use for something you could get again, throw it out. Also, if you haven't looked at a piece of paper for six months and it's just lying in a drawer, throw it out. You should also review your files at least once a year to make certain you're not holding on to a lot of unnecessary paper."

Here are a number of other helpful hints that can help you reduce a potentially overwhelming quantity of paper. If this has been a chronic problem, it might help to make a copy of this list and hang it up near your desk (uh oh, not another piece of paper!):

The Paper Diet

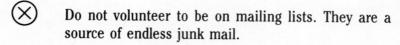 Do not volunteer to be on mailing lists. They are a source of endless junk mail.

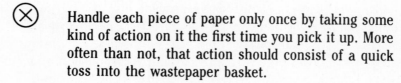 Handle each piece of paper only once by taking some kind of action on it the first time you pick it up. More often than not, that action should consist of a quick toss into the wastepaper basket.

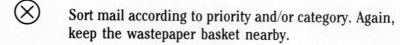 Sort mail according to priority and/or category. Again, keep the wastepaper basket nearby.

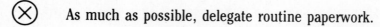 As much as possible, delegate routine paperwork.

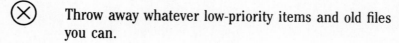 Throw away whatever low-priority items and old files you can.

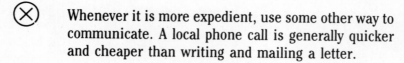 Whenever it is more expedient, use some other way to communicate. A local phone call is generally quicker and cheaper than writing and mailing a letter.

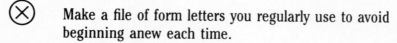 Make a file of form letters you regularly use to avoid beginning anew each time.

Is paper just one of the things you tend to accumulate too much of? The same people who are swamped with obsolete and useless paper often have similar problems getting rid of all kinds of things, be it clothing, furniture, or whatever. Here's how Maggie Cadman explains this dynamic:

"Some people are afraid to throw out anything they own, no matter how useless it might be. They feel that if they get rid of those things, they somehow won't be as solid to themselves or have as much reality to themselves as they do with all that junk around. The truth is, people feel more solid and real after they get rid of all their superfluous things because they have a much greater feeling of mastery over their surroundings. If you haven't used something in six months to a year, give it away as a tax deduction, put it in storage—just get it out of your house or workspace."

The importance of records

While you're getting down to throwing out all that useless paper and other junk that's been cluttering up your workspace, there's one kind of paperwork you should probably consider increasing—records that pertain to your business. When you work for yourself it is essential that you keep accurate and detailed records of your suppliers, contacts, clients, bright ideas, and everything else that affects your business. The purpose of such organizational devices is, as we have noted at the front of this section, to make your life less (not more) encumbered by detail.

Let's assume for a moment that you are a graphic designer who gets called to do an unusual, but very well-paying job. The materials you require must be obtained from suppliers other than the ones you generally deal with. Also, you need to subcontract two other artists who specialize in particular areas needed to execute the design. The job is a success and well worth your time. Two years later, another client who saw your work calls you up for a similar job. You are eager to take on the project, but since you kept no records, you don't remember which suppliers and artists you used or exactly how much you charged. Had you maintained such records, you could simply refer to them every time a similar situation came up. Within a matter of moments, you would be reminded about every detail relating to the project, including: your profit, names and costs of suppliers and subcontractees, terms of billing, and any special problems that might have arisen. Without records, however, you are at the complete mercy of your memory.

Another important reason to invest a bit of time in maintaining good records is to avoid crisis or high-stress situations. In Chapter Three, we discussed the absolute necessity of maintaining accurate financial records as a freelancer. What would happen if you didn't bother maintaining such records and the IRS called you in for an audit just as you were in the midst of working around the clock to complete an important deadline? This kind of crisis could put you under a tremendous emotional strain at a time when you really needed to direct your energies into your work. Or, what if a client who accepted a piece of work you completed was suddenly refusing to pay you, and you couldn't locate the signed purchase order?

Remember, as a self-employed person, you create all the systems that keep your business running. In the final analysis, the most important person in your record-keeping scheme is not Uncle Sam, but you! It's possible that one day the tax auditor is going to want to know how you spent your time and how much it cost. Then again, you may never get audited. On the other hand, you can be absolutely certain that you will need accurate records to tell you what took place in the past in order to make more informed business decisions in the future.

How Productive Are You?

Perhaps you are the kind of person who likes to "hang loose," and you resent having to place any time constrictions on yourself. We've seen freelancers become exasperated and say, "If I wanted to deal with rigid routines, I'd get myself a nine-to-five job." Indeed, freelancers who don't get a handle on their use of time may well find themselves punching a clock for someone else before long. As we've said before: Successful self-employment hinges on balancing freedom with responsibility. You may have a lot more flexibility in how you use your time than your friends who work nine-to-five, but this flexibility does not mean that you don't have to ask yourself the same kinds of bottom-line questions as any business person. In relation to your finances, the bottom line question is: How much of a profit did you make? In terms of time, the relevant question is: How productive have you been?

Management consultant Michael LeBoeuf envisions personal productivity as a measurable commodity:

$$\text{Personal Productivity} = \frac{\text{What you produce}}{\substack{\text{The number of hours it takes} \\ \text{you to produce it}^7}}$$

Does this kind of mathematical approach to your use of time seem a bit cold and scientific? Well, it is. By employing a formula like this, you can take an objective look at how well you're utilizing those precious hours. Let's assume you are a self-employed cabinetmaker who takes on a job for $1,000. When you add up all the time it took to complete that job, you find that it amounted to a total of fifty hours to produce that cabinet. Could you have been more productive? The answer harks back to issues we discussed earlier in this chapter, namely:

○ Did you schedule various tasks for the most suitable times?

○ Did you delegate low-priority, low-value tasks?

○ Did you have other projects going that hindered your work on this one?

○ Did you procrastinate at one or more points while completing the project?

○ Were you well organized in terms of materials and workspace to facilitate completion of the job?

○ Did your fee accurately reflect the number of hours needed to finish the job?

Any improvement you could make in these areas can cut down the number of hours it takes to complete the project, thus increasing your productivity. What are the benefits of improving your productivity? Greater profits for one. You don't need to be a mathematical genius to see that by cutting down on the number of hours required to build the cabinet, you would increase your per-hour profit. The more productive you are, the more money you make.

By completing your work in less time, you've got additional hours available for leisure activities, vacations, or whatever. If you're a cabinetmaker, and you can cut the time it takes to create your product down from fifty to forty hours, you can spend that extra time building another cabinet, working on a completely unrelated project, or sleeping on the beach. The point is simple: *By making more productive use of time, you automatically decrease working hours and increase profits.*

A QUASI-INSPIRATIONAL MESSAGE ON IMPROVED TIME MANAGEMENT

OKAY, YOU'VE READ THE CHAPTER AND DEtermined to do everything in your power to make more productive use of your time—or have you? We're aware that some of the long-standing habits that underlie poor time management are not so easy to change. Not to worry. We're not looking for any major miracles here. If you can gradually incorporate just a few of the principles we've discussed over a period of time, you can become far more productive in your work. Little things like delegating unimportant tasks or utilizing an answering machine to screen out interruptions can eventually spur you on to greater heights in becoming a brilliant time artist. People who have instituted such seemingly minor improvements have gotten such dramatic results that they become hungry for other relatively painless ways to get more out of their time. Here are twenty tips that can help you manage your time better. Pick one or two and use them as your starting point. Do it *now*! Time's a'wasting!

1. Always ask yourself: What can I do right now to move toward my goals?

2. Know exactly what you're doing and why.

3. Concentrate fully on the matter at hand.

4. Work with as much energy and enthusiasm as you can muster.

5. Know when you are working and when you are not working.

6. Spend as much time as possible on priorities.

7. Delegate as much as possible.

8. Eliminate procrastination and Implementation Time.

9. Define your goals and specific motivators.

10. Think of the time spent waiting in lines and in office waiting rooms as an opportunity to get some work done.

11. Invest some time improving your health. This will save you time feeling fatigued and taking care of illness.

12. Keep your long-term goals in mind, even while you're engaged in seemingly menial tasks.

13. Pinpoint your most productive times of the day and use them to maximum benefit.

14. Set deadlines by committing to others.

15. Avoid interruptions whenever possible.

16. Learn how to say *no* and *good-bye*.

17. Know how long things take, and add on some additional time.

18. Seek out high-quality leisure and creative rest time.

19. Plan your day around anchors and routines.

20. Try to add another timesaving technique to your repertoire each week.

7

BRINGING IT OUT INTO THE WORLD: A Short Course in Marketing for People Who Work for Themselves

Up until now, we've been exploring the kinds of things you can do on your own to improve your businesses. Formulating goals, controlling finances, developing productive habits, and using time effectively are all valuable components of any freelancer's success. But there is an overriding consideration that puts everything that has come before into a critical perspective. You must bring your skills out into the world if you are going to make it.

You can be the most talented, highly motivated, well-organized freelancer on the planet, but the question is: Can you turn all of that into something that the world recognizes and rewards? Unless you can get people interested in what you do, all of your efforts probably won't amount to very much.

Many self-employed people work alone, but none live in a vacuum. No matter how hard we may fight it, we all want our efforts to get out there and float. In spite of this, some freelancers don't want to touch the world too often. They find it scary and threatening, and compared to hiding in their safe little shell, it is! Outside there are people who will let you know if all your hard work really amounts to anything. They will tell you if your work is worth buying and how much you will be paid for it. In the final analysis, what *they* say and do has at least as much impact on your career as what you say and do. Think about it: *In order to reap financial profit and recognition in your career you need to generate a consistent amount of income-producing work.* This realization is the first step of what we call an "Ongoing Marketing Program." If you are interested in bringing your work out into the marketplace, you need to take stock of the following:

- **Who you are and what you do**

- **Who your clients are and what they need**

- **What's going on with your competition**

In order to survive and thrive on your own, you are going to have to defeat financial insecurity—that merciless killer of the self-employed. Money may not buy you health, but it can buy health insurance, retirement programs, and all those other nice little perks nine-to-fivers enjoy. If you've got enough money coming in consistently, you can overcome many of the drawbacks struggling freelancers complain about. You can make this happen, but first you've got to get out into the world and show people what you can do.

We understand that most people who work for themselves were never schooled in the fine points of marketing themselves. When you come right down to it, though, becoming a good self-marketer is pretty much the same as becoming good at anything else you do. It takes practice and experience. How did you become good at your work? Perhaps you started out with some knowledge and basic skills; then you refined those skills by doing whatever it is you do over and over again. In the same way, you

Some freelancers are reluctant to go out into the "Real World."

can become good at marketing—by starting out with some basic guidelines and applying them continuously in your dealings. A successful marketing program can do wonders for your financial situation and provide positive answers to these other vital questions:

☞ How much recognition will you receive for your work?

☞ What kind of a lifestyle will you enjoy?

☞ Will you reach your career potential?

☞ Will you achieve your long-range objectives?

223

THREE ATTITUDES TOWARD MARKETING YOURSELF

One: I've Got the Goods; Come and Get Me

Have you ever read about those Hollywood parties where beautiful actors and actresses just stand around waiting to be discovered? We know freelancers in all industries who take that same kind of attitude. In essence they are saying: "I'm so fantastically talented, my work ought to sell itself." People with this approach somehow feel that it is demeaning to take an active role in marketing their talents. This attitude has prevented many talented freelancers from reaching their potential. We'd all like to think that we're so talented and have so much to offer, we can just sit back and wait while the world beats a path to our door. That just ain't the way it happens. You've got to put a sign on your door to let people know that the goods are there and seek out those customers who won't even get to see that sign on their own. Maybe if you were the only game in town, things would be a little different—though at the very least, you would still have to let people know you are in business.

As it is, most of us work in highly competitive fields where a client can pick and choose those freelancers he (or she) finds most desirable. What do you suppose will make him select you for a particular job?

Here are some of the things that clients take into consideration, but in order for them to find these things out about you you've got to get out there.

☐ They like you and would enjoy working with you.

☐ They consider you an expert at this job.

☐ You are easy to work with.

☐ You will enhance the assignment beyond what is asked for.

☐ You will deliver what you promise when you promise it.

☐ You are on the same wavelength as the client and truly understand his needs.

These considerations are crucial during the early stages of your career when you are trying to establish a foothold, but they are also important for even the most successful businesses. Have you noticed that top authors and recording artists appear on as many talk shows as possible for little or no compensation when they're trying to promote a new release? They know that if they don't keep themselves in front of the public they will be forgotten.

This same principle applies to mega corporations like Coca-Cola. Though they've been the largest selling soft drink for years, they still maintain a vigorous marketing program. All those TV ads aren't just tax write-offs. The people who run Coca-Cola know that if they slack off in their marketing, they'll be overtaken by Pepsi or some other soft drink. Question: If these giants of their industries find it necessary to devote time and effort to marketing, how important are these considerations for the rest of us?

"I know that I should get my ass out there more," a freelance financial consultant named James told us, "but I just hate the thought of having to sell myself." When we asked James what the term "selling myself" means to him, he mentioned the stereotyped image of a cigar-chomping, fast-talking used-car salesman and the distasteful notion of prostituting himself. "Think about the way those words sound," he added. "Selling yourself!"

We understand Jim's point of view, but we look at it a bit differently. A buyer-seller relationship works on a value-for-value basis. When you work for yourself, you provide your client with something he needs, and he gives you income, which you need. You both need each other to exist. But in a market where there are more suppliers than buyers, it is up to you to pursue the client. Even in a market where there were more clients than suppliers to service them, you would need to take steps to make people aware of you. In competitive fields, you are going to require more than a minimal effort. In order to make it, you need to commit yourself to an ongoing marketing effort that includes the following activities:

Marketing Activities Anyone Can Use

$ Calls to clients and contacts

$ Calls to secondary sources (libraries, trade organizations) for information on the field

$ Mailings to clients and contacts about what you are doing

$ Mailings relating to clients and contacts to serve as reminders you are out there—to keep you in mind

$ Social activities, such as lunches, dinners with clients and contacts

$ Research in libraries and trade organizations to get information.

Ironically, it is the truly talented individuals who suffer most when they don't take their work out into the world. If you really have something the world wants and you're just sitting in your room with it, you've got a lot more to lose than if you had little or no talent. While you sit around hoping for a miracle, someone else is out there getting the work.

One talented songwriter we know simply refuses to take his songs around to publishers and recording artists. He stubbornly clings to the notion that if his work never surfaces, it will be the world's loss, not his own. But, in fact, the world cannot lose that which it is unaware of. The public will find other good songs to listen to and our songwriter friend (who drives a taxi for a living) will have a closet full of his unknown "hits." Who do you think the real loser is in this situation?

Two: I'm Not Going to Make It Unless I Get Work

Self-employed people who stay afloat for a few years develop some basic selling skills almost without trying. They have gone through times when work is coming in and times when they can hardly make ends meet. Periodically, they find it necessary to go out and scrape up some work. Because they have been at it for a while, they have established enough contacts and clients to survive by making some calls and setting up some appointments as the need arises. But is survival enough? When you are at the beginning of your career, it may be exciting to discover that you can actually get by working for yourself. But excitement eventually turns to drudgery if survival is all you are reaping. Check your goals: Are you in business just to make ends meet or are you striving to make financial and creative progress as you become more experienced? It may sound like a cliché, but if you stand still for any length of time, you are, in effect, losing ground.

Some freelancers explain their minimal selling efforts by pointing to rather modest financial objectives. "Money isn't everything," they say. But consider this: The more well-known and well paid you are in your field, the more freedom you have to progress in creative areas of your work. This point was recently driven home by an article on David Geffen—the young entertainment industry wiz.

After numerous successes in launching his own record companies and producing hit plays like *Dreamgirls*, Geffen signed a deal with Warner Records that gives him virtually "unlimited access to Warner funds." When Mo Ostin, chairman of Warner Records, was asked why such an unprecedented deal was made, he said: "A winner like David . . . you gotta bet on. Someone like that, he's driven. He's just gotta succeed. You know that whatever he touches is going to turn to gold."[1]

There are very few David Geffens in any field. Yet each of us in our own way wants to have the freedom and the resources to do whatever we want in our work, but this requires building credibility in graduated steps. Unless we begin by letting potential customers know what we can do, we can't even begin to climb that ladder.

Three: The Ongoing Marketing Approach

Successful freelancers agee that a good deal of the stress and uncertainty of their working lives was greatly reduced once they started earning a consistently good living. In most cases, this is not accomplished by a sudden windfall, but a continuous effort to bring their talents out into the world. As one writer put it: "It is the nature of the freelance beast that in order to keep eating (and eating well), it must constantly seek work."

Organizational consultant Maggie Cadman finds that such an ongoing approach has particular impact in highly competitive fields such as acting:

> "I find that people who do something for their career every day do make progress. It's rough when you're in an overcrowded field like acting. People get discouraged quickly because they know there are so many others out there trying to do the same thing. It's easy to say, 'It's a meat market out there, and my hands are tied,' but that's actually not true. Some of my clients read all the trades, go to auditions, write thank-you notes, and call people when they say they are going to call. If you have talent and do these other things consistently, you will get results."

People who market themselves continuously aren't endowed with any special talents. After a while, these techniques just become a regular part of their routine.

A young writer noted that Chris, a successful nonfiction author, seemed to devote hardly any of her time to marketing herself, yet she was one of the better-known writers in her field.

"But you're wrong," Chris chimed in after overhearing the remark. "I do all kinds of things to keep myself working. I read trade papers, send out proposals, speak with other writers and editors, attend informal gatherings where I often meet others in my field or people who can give me work. I also belong to several professional organizations in which I take an active role. I've been doing these things for so long, though, that they do seem almost effortless. Still, the majority of the things I do won't generate any work for me, but that small percentage of my efforts that does turn into something tangible forms the basis for whatever success I've had."

Not all successful freelancers find their marketing activities to be quite so effortless as Chris does. However, this doesn't stop them from pushing ahead.

We recently ran into a well-known writer of music for commercials in the waiting room of a major advertising agency.

Holding up a briefcase full of demo tapes, he confessed: "I really don't like this part of my work that much. I'd much rather be in the studio working on the music. I went through a period when I had far more work than I could handle. I was working around the clock to finish all my assignments and totally stopped going to see people. Suddenly, I finished my assignments and there was no new work coming in. When I called my clients, they said: 'We didn't know you were available, so we called someone else.' Now I make it my business to go see a few people every week, no matter how much work I have. There are too many other qualified people out there for me to tune out this aspect of my business. I'm starting to realize that it's something I'll always have to pay a certain amount of attention to."

The amount of effort you put into marketing activities depends on where you are in your career. If you are just starting out, you probably need to proceed more vigorously than those who are more established (like anything else you do, the hardest work usually comes at the beginning). Once you've built a good reputation in your industry, it becomes much easier to keep on the right track by using gentle marketing devices like follow-up calls and reminders to clients.

Your Batting Average

If you follow baseball, you know that a .300 batting average is considered top-notch. Actually, a .300 hitter is unsuccessful 70 percent of the time, but in his field, three hits out of every ten at bats is considered an excellent percentage. We think freelancers benefit greatly by approaching their marketing efforts the same way. Too many beginners get discouraged after they strike out once or twice, not realizing that each time they go to bat, their chances for a hit improve: The freelancer who makes twenty phone calls a week to potential clients has a better chance of landing an assignment than the one who only makes two calls. People who maintain an ongoing marketing approach get lots of "at bats" over the years and improve their chances to get more hits. The reasons for this do not only lie in sheer numbers, but in what you learn each time you come up to bat. As Adele Scheele puts it: *It is only through repeated efforts in experimentation and risk-taking that we achieve the confidence and awareness that enable us to approach people in an appropriate way [and] ask for what we want.*[2]

What Part Does Marketing Play in Your Career?

In order to develop an ongoing marketing approach that suits you, you must recognize its place in your total scheme of things. If you've completed some of the exercises in previous chapters, you already have some indication of your marketing needs. For example, if your definition of success involves making more money, that's a strong hint that you need to spend more time *bringing it out into the world*. Here are some other questions to help you evaluate how your current marketing program fits into the overall picture:

1. Do you only work on improving your craft and believe that the world will come to you?

2. Do you do some marketing activity every day?

3. Is this activity enough to create the right kind of movement toward your goals?

4. Do you set aside a regular time for calls and mailings?

5. Which habits do you need to improve to have more regular marketing activity?

6. Would a continuous marketing plan help you reach your goals faster and more effectively?

7. Do you see marketing activities as a priority?

8. Which specific tool do you need to use more in your marketing? (a) calling; (b) research; (c) mailings; (d) social?

PRESENTATION: Who Are You and What Do You Do?

> The purpose of self-presentation is to act in our own best interest, and act as though we are the successful people that we want to be.
>
> Adele Scheele[3]

Who are you? That's a simple enough question. Or maybe it really isn't so simple after all. If you want to get philosophical about it, you can probably spend a lifetime pondering the existential implications of this one question. On the other hand, when you call someone about work or go see them in their office, you may only get a few minutes to let that person know who you are. In fact, you can make a lasting first impression in a matter of seconds, so you want that initial communication to be a positive one. This is true in all areas of life, but it is particularly important for freelancers communicating with clients. For whatever reasons, many buyers have a less-than-glowing impression of the independent contractors with whom they deal. That's why you want to be highly professional in your communications. Ask yourself if you are presenting the best you in all your dealings—from your résumé and business cards to the way you handle yourself on the phone with secretaries to the kinds of clothes you wear when you go see clients.

How important is the creation of a professional image for freelancers? We believe it to be crucial, though we've seen many of our contemporaries sorely neglect these areas. "I've been trying to update my portfolio and design a new business card for years," an illustrator named Paul told us, "but I'm so tied up with my work that I just haven't gotten a chance." When we suggested that perhaps the deficiencies in his presentation were preventing him from making more money, Paul answered: "You might be right, but I think it's more important for me to concentrate on the creative aspects of my work."

Advertisements for Yourself

In its own way, effective self-presentation can require as much creativity as your actual work. Think of how much money businesses pay advertising agencies to create an image that the public will buy. In a sense, you must learn to act as your own advertising agency if you want to convince clients to give you work. Once you view self-presentation as an ongoing advertising program for yourself, you can begin looking at how you communicate from the point of view of those who hire and refer you to others. Market research consultant and former president of the New York chapter of the American Marketing Association, Newton Frank, puts it this way:

> "In order to get hired, you have to decide what you really want to get across and do that convincingly. Presenting yourself in a manner that is convincing leads to the next step in the mind of the buyer. It causes him to ask—'*Can I make use of this person and for what?*'"

In order to convince a buyer to make use of your services, you must be able to communicate specifically what you can do for him. This seemingly simple task is one that baffles many freelancers, particularly those who possess a variety of talents within a field. It is only natural to want to let people know as many aspects of your work as possible. On the other hand, such an approach discounts the fact that most people in a position to hire you are very busy. Put yourself in the shoes of a potential client. He or she probably has a number of projects on his mind at any given time. He's also got lots to remember plus the usual variety of personal pressures. Suddenly this freelancer he may never have seen before walks in looking for work. How can you penetrate everything else that's going on in his life?

Al Ries, co-author of the book *Positioning*, and chairman of the board of the advertising agency Trout & Ries, feels that the best way to get your message to stand out is to "select the material that has the best chance of getting through." Ries believes that freelancers face many of the same problems attracting customers as advertisers: i.e., a highly competitive society in which people are barraged by an enormous volume of communication. He suggests that freelancers simplify their presentations in order to "cut through the traffic jam in the prospect's mental highway."[4]

"I believe that it's very important for freelancers to be as specific as possible with the customer in communicating what they do. Too many people say, 'If you've got a problem, call me.' They try to be all things to all people. It's hard for them to appreciate the advantages of reducing everything down to one single, simple concept. . . . That's difficult in a way because you have to throw part of your expertise out in a sense. But I find that the more general you are, the less people perceive you as an expert.

"For instance, if I'm a surgeon and you need an eye operation, whom will you select, me or the eye specialist? . . . The same principle applies to freelancing. I hire freelance artists from time to time. When they come in to see me, I'll ask them, 'What do you do?' They'll often say, 'I'll do anything.' That virtually assures that they

won't get hired. On the other hand, if a freelancer walks
in here and says, 'I do eight-page, four-color brochures,'
the next time I had an eight-page, four-color brochure,
I'd know who to call."

Trout & Ries call the process of being selective in your
communications and narrowing your targets *positioning*. This is a
particularly important process when you are trying to get your
foot in the door. Once a client has experience dealing with you,
he may hire you for an assignment in another area. But when you
walk in looking for your first assignment, make sure you give that
potential client something simple and specific to hang his hat on.
If you have several areas that you are equally adept in, make sure
you have separate presentations prepared for each. This may
necessitate making up several résumés or selecting different samples for your portfolio. Try to find out what the potential client's
needs are and gear your presentation accordingly. Also, keep in
mind that if you make a favorable impression on a potential
client, he might hire you at a later date even if he can't use your
services immediately.

What Do You Do?

Are your communications concise enough to
get across? We find that freelancers often have difficulty answering the simple question: "What do you do?" Since this is so
fundamental to presenting yourself, we suggest that you do the
following exercise:

☆   Write one paragraph describing what you do.

☆   If you have more than one specialty, write a paragraph for
each.

☆ Keeping in mind that you often have only a very short time to get your message across, reduce each of your paragraphs to one or two sentences.

To help you with this exercise, look at the five sets of clear and unclear (less specific) statements that appear below and review your own descriptions accordingly:

1. *Clear:* I raise funds for nonprofit organizations in the arts.
   Unclear: I do various tasks for lots of different kinds of organizations.

2. *Clear:* I design educational software programs for use on personal computers that handle up to 64K memory.
   Unclear: I'm into computers.

3. *Clear:* I'm a freelance market research consultant with expertise in doing industry surveys for the food industry.
   Unclear: I do consulting for corporations.

4. *Clear:* I write fiction books for the teen market, with an emphasis on adventure stories for boys and girls.
   Unclear: I'm a writer.

5. *Clear:* I'm a troubleshooter for clothing manufacturers. I find out how their business operates—all facets—and then make concrete suggestions on where they can cut costs without sacrificing quality.
   Unclear: I can do whatever you need.

The more specific you are about describing what you do, the easier you make it for the person in the position to hire you to do so. Somebody is going to get the assignment, why not you?

It would be a shame to lose a job you were qualified for just because your communication was poor or inconcise. Once you've taken the time to find out what a particular client is looking for, you ought to be able to gear your presentation accordingly. But don't be *so* flexible or eager for work that it hinders your professional image. You can't be something you're not, so try to highlight those things you do best.

What Are Your Clients Looking For?

No matter what it is you do and how skilled you are at communicating it, there are a number of general attributes that clients in all businesses look for when they hire freelancers. These include:

•*Expertise*. When someone hires you, they want to feel that they are giving you an assignment you've tackled a thousand times. Al Ries notes that freelancers often try to build themselves up by indicating to the client that the job at hand is a tremendous challenge. That's not what clients want to hear. They want to believe that you can handle the work without a hitch. "The credibility factor is very important," notes Ries. "If you want to look like an expert, make things look easy, not hard. Someone who does things with ease looks a hell of a lot better and more competent than someone who is struggling."

•*Honesty*. Clients want to feel that they are dealing with someone who will level with them. If you do run into some kind of major snag or problem in delivery, the client wants to be confident you will communicate this to him.

•*Personableness*. Never forget that your clients are people. Like you, they respond to a certain amount of friendliness and personal contact. Also, they want to work with people who are easy to deal with. We've seen too many freelancers deliver a fantastic job and never get hired again because the client perceived them as being too difficult to get along with.

•*Independence*. Clients don't really want to know about freelancers' financial problems. If a regular client tells you that he has no work this month, it would be inappropriate for you to say, "But how am I going to pay my rent?" Not only isn't this the client's problem, it weakens your position in his eyes. Never let a client think you depend on him, even if you do.

•*Value added*. Clients often want to feel that you are likely to deliver quality beyond the stated terms of your agreement. They may settle for delivery of a satisfactory job, but they are hoping you can deliver a superior job, or perhaps offer a suggestion that enhances the overall quality of the finished product.

Self-Presentation: Some Common Questions

As we've said before, experience is the greatest teacher of self-presentation skills. There are few really hard and fast rules, though there are some basic guidelines such as the ones we've been exploring. Space limitations prevent us from addressing all the questions that pertain to these issues, but here are some of the things that frequently come up in our consultations and seminars:

Phone calls

—"I enjoy talking to friends but I'm uncomfortable making business calls. Is there any way to get around this?"

Calling is often the first step in presenting yourself. Some freelancers have an agent or rep, but it is nearly impossible to circumvent the telephone in marketing yourself. After doing it for a while, you learn to take a more relaxed, social attitude when you make business calls. Potential clients are often as uncomfortable as you are. Don't forget, they are also talking to someone they don't know. If you come across in an open, friendly manner, you'll find that people will tend to respond in kind.

* * *

—**"Whenever I call anyone important, I only get through to a secretary, who usually tells me that the person I'm trying to reach is tied up. When this happens, I tend to get frustrated and a bit hostile. What can I do about this?"**

In most businesses, it is unusual to get through to powerful people directly. One of the perks of power is having your calls screened so that you don't have to waste time with unwanted phone calls. Secretaries serve as screeners for phone calls, but remember, a dependable, experienced secretary is often given complete discretion of who gets through and who doesn't. If a secretary is speaking to a freelancer for the first time, she (or he) may relay her first impression to her boss. You will get much further if you go out of your way to be courteous and friendly to secretaries. Learn their names and make sure they know yours. If you come on with a negative attitude, you may never get through.

* * *

—**"What do I do when a secretary says that her boss will call me back in a few minutes, and two days later my call hasn't been returned? Will I be perceived as being pushy if I keep trying?"**

In the world of business, secretaries will almost always tell you that the person you are trying to reach will get back to you. In some cases, that person has no intention of returning your call, but, for the most part, he or she is probably just too busy with pressing matters and hasn't gotten around to it. Freelancers sometimes take this to mean that they are powerless and unimportant while the person they are trying to reach is somehow omnipotent. This is not the case. Ultimately, any client who buys your services needs those services just as much as you need the work. You probably don't know what that potential client's priorities are at a given time but if one of your priorities is to get in touch with him or her, it is part of your job to pursue that.

Don't take it personally if someone doesn't call you back when they say they will, and don't hesitate to try again for fear you'll be thought of as pushy.

As a supplier, part of your job is to make clients aware of your services so they can hire you. At the same time, people who employ you expect to be called and reminded. They don't want to be nagged, but they expect to be pursued.

We were in the office of a successful business manager who was trying to get in touch with a company president to close a deal on behalf of a client. This business manager takes great pride in his ability to get through to the most powerful people in his business at any time. Still, this particular company president clearly did not want to speak to the business manager at that moment. Not to be deterred, the business manager called every five minutes and spoke to a secretary.

"He just went to the bathroom," the secretary reported. "Call back in five minutes."

The business manager waited a few minutes, then called back. "Is he off the pot yet?" he asked the secretary.

This went on for the next half hour. The business manager hadn't yet reached the president of the company, but he kept calling back every five minutes or so. Apparently, he wasn't worried in the least about intruding or making a pest of himself. We're not advising you to pursue clients with this sort of vigor, but neither should you feel overly hesitant about taking care of business.

*　　*　　*

Appropriate dress

—"Do I always have to dress formally for business appointments?"

It all depends on the business you're in and how you want to be perceived. If you're a systems analyst seeking a consulting assignment at a bank, you should wear a suit. In this situation, even a well-tailored sports jacket and slacks for men would probably be too informal. In other industries, however, the dress code can be radically different. In record companies, for example, executives often wear jeans and a tee shirt. If a musician walked in with a blue suit and tie, that might be an indication that he or she was unfamiliar with the industry. One jingle singer we know arrived at a session dressed in a business suit. The clients wanted him to sing with a country and western twang in his voice. Although the singer was adept at this musical style, the clients kept saying that somehow his performance just wasn't convincing. The next day he walked in with jeans and a western shirt and everyone just loved his performance.

The way you look is an important part of your presentation, no matter what line of work you're in. The clothes you wear are simply another advertisement for who you are. As we've noted, it is possible to overdress. But more often than not, freelancers tend to dress too casually. Find out what people in your industry expect from their business associates. Don't dress so casually that you erode your professional image in the client's mind. Remem-

Dress appropriately

ber, many corporate types don't hold freelancers in the highest esteem. By dressing appropriately, you show that you are serious about your career and the business at hand.

*   *   *

Materials

—"Should I change the work samples in my portfolio to suit different clients?"

Absolutely! Your portfolio is a physical representation of what you do. Quite frequently, you will be asked to leave it so the client can scrutinize it at his or her leisure. In that case, your portfolio must speak for itself. Some freelancers put together portfolios on the basis of what they consider to be their best work, rather than what the client is looking for. Before you decide which work samples to present, find out something about the client and what his or her needs are. If you're a graphic designer looking for work designing corporate brochures, don't put prints of your abstract paintings in your portfolio.

The work samples you present to clients can be your best sales rep. They can demonstrate your talent as well as your sensitivity to the marketplace. We recommend that you spend as much time as necessary custom tailoring your presentation when you go out to find work. This is especially true for people who are experienced in a number of related areas. Show clients those samples which will make them say "This person is exactly what I'm looking for." And keep in mind that clients are usually looking for something quite specific. They want to hire people who can solve specific problems for them.

*   *   *

—"Do all freelancers need business cards and letterheads?"

We recommend that one of the first things to do when you go into business is to get a business card and letterhead. For most people, these are relatively inexpensive items that can usually be obtained within a few days. If you are in the visual arts, however, your materials will probably need to be more elaborate. In these instances, the medium is the message. If you are an illustrator, you will probably want to create some kind of logo that actually demonstrates your skills. For the rest of us, however, the main purpose of these materials is to present ourselves as legitimately established professionals.

People at the beginning of their careers tend to be penny wise and dollar foolish about these things. They tell themselves that they'll wait until their cash flow is better before shelling out the money for business cards and stationery. This kind of thinking can destroy opportunities for you before they ever open up. Let's say you run into a potentially important contact at a social function who asks for your card. Not only do you look unprofessional when you say you don't have one, but after you scribble your name and number on some scrap of paper, you can hardly expect the potential contact to treat it with the same regard he would a professional printed card. The same thing applies to letterheads. When you correspond with a client, you hardly come across as a going concern if you don't have a letterhead. If that piece of correspondence is a letter of introduction, the client isn't going to be very favorably impressed with a freelancer who can't afford stationery. So do yourself a favor: Spend the fifty or one hundred bucks and get these materials as soon as you possibly can.

*   *   *

—"Do I need a résumé to get work?"

We know a number of people who have gone through their entire career without a résumé. In some fields, clients are only interested in your work samples, so résumés aren't important. Still, we don't think it can hurt to have one. A résumé is useful as a short introductory statement of what you do. It gives a client the opportunity to decide whether you've got the qualifications for the job. If you have more than one specialty, we recommend that you develop a résumé for each one. Perhaps the best reason for having a résumé is simply that it is a self-presentation tool you may be asked for at any time. Therefore, if you are questioning whether or not you need one, you probably do.

WHAT'S GOING ON OUT THERE?

TRULY IT WOULD BE A SHAME IF YOU SPENT ALL that time getting your presentation together, only to find that no one was interested. Self-presentation is the "me" side of communication. It answers the question: How well am I coming across to others? There is a flip side to that question which is just as important and that is: *Who are the people I am trying to reach, and what are they looking for?* The better you can answer these questions, the greater your chances of improving your business.

All self-employed people need to know what's going on in the marketplace. To the extent that you seek out and analyze this information, you engage in market research. To proceed without feedback from the marketplace is to deprive yourself of vital knowledge. Jeannie, a fifty-year-old woman who attended one of our seminars, related a particularly poignant story that underscores the need to know as much as you can about your business.

Look Before You Leap

Jeannie had worked for twenty years for one company as a semiskilled laborer. All that time, she saved regularly so that she could open a business of her own. When she finally socked away enough money, she bought a dress shop in a residential neighborhood. The shop had been a going concern for twelve years, and Jeannie noticed that business was quite brisk, especially on weekends. She felt this was a great opportunity to fulfill her dream, and she bought the dress shop for cash. Though she had no previous business experience, Jeannie did not take the trouble to find out what she was getting into. By the time she attended our seminar, about a year later, Jeannie had acquired certain information which may well have prevented her from buying that business in the first place.

"I didn't know this before, but there are a number of companies selling similar dresses door to door for less money in the neighborhood. This has been going on for a long time, but I didn't know about it when I bought the store. Also, there are a couple of large department stores a few blocks away that offer greater selection and lower prices. Although business is pretty good on weekends, it is quite slow during the week. Unfortunately, I only passed by on Saturdays and Sundays when I was working at my job, and I didn't get a realistic picture of how well they were doing. Right now, I've got to work twelve hours a day, seven days a week, just to break even. Hopefully, things will improve, but right now I'm working much harder for far less money than when I was an employee."

Actually, Jeannie's story isn't as tragic as it might be. All things considered, she's pretty lucky to break even. There were all kinds of things she could have done to get a more complete picture of what she was getting into *before* she risked her life savings. She could have made it a point to check out the store at different times and on different days of the week. She could have spoken with local consumers and merchants; she could have looked at local newspapers and seen the ads for shop-at-home dresses; and finally, she could have consulted with an accountant or lawyer and asked for counsel. Unfortunately, she chose not to do any of these things. All she knew was that she wanted her own business and she was going to buy it with no questions asked.

Know Your Business

Jeannie's story might seem extreme, but we've seen too many cases of people who don't look before they leap. Even if we don't normally invest our life savings, we all invest time, money, and energy in what we're doing. Remember the concept of opportunity cost that we discussed in relation to finances? Whenever you choose to do something, you are giving up the opportunities you might gain by doing something else. That's why it is so essential to find out as much as you can about your potential clients and everything else that affects your business. By systematically searching out and analyzing information about the marketplace, you will be able to:

○ Communicate more effectively with clients

○ Make better business decisions

○ Reduce the cost of uncertainty by saving time and money.

You and Sherlock Holmes

How good a detective are you? Show us someone who knows how to be at the right place at the right time with the right solutions to his or her customers' needs, and we'll show you a skilled private eye. There are lots of clues that can help you make better business decisions if you'll only take full advantage of them. Here are some suggestions:

WHERE TO LOOK FOR CLUES:

▶ Friends, relatives, and other contacts who work in your business or related fields

▶ Professional societies, organizations, unions, and guilds

▶ Attorneys, accountants, and other specialists who serve your industry

▶ Informal groups and networks of freelancers in your field

▶ The Bureau of Labor Statistics

▶ Trade publications (listed in the *Encyclopedia of Associations*)

▶ Standard and Poor's industry surveys

▶ Public libraries (especially ones with good reference sections)

▶ Reference librarians (they often know where to find the specific information you need)

▶ Potential customers

Just as the great fictional detective heroes always get their man, the less renowned, but similarly heroic freelance-detectives always land the assignment (well, maybe not always, but a lot more often than their less inquisitive counterparts). We've indicated some of the places to search out clues. Here are five essential questions they can help you answer:

Who are your customers?

Before you do anything else, you should make a list of every potential customer for your product. We are amazed at how many beginning freelancers overlook this obvious first step. Then again, this kind of attitude goes hand in hand with the *"I've got the goods, come and get me"* approach to marketing. If you want to find work, put on your detective cap and search out your potential customers. If you're a writer, there is an annual edition of *Writer's Market*, which lists virtually every publishing house in America, the kinds of things they are interested in, and even their procedures for handling proposals. If you're looking for work in the music industry, *Billboard* and *Cashbox* print yearbooks that list most major record companies and song publishers. Many industries offer these kinds of publications. If yours doesn't, check your local library or contact the Bureau of Labor Statistics. Remember, your potential customers are not trying to hide. They need suppliers or they won't be able to turn out finished products. Even the richest companies in the most competitive industries cannot afford to close their doors to new talent.

Where are your customers located?

We've seen self-employed people struggle unnecessarily because they were not located advantageously to deal with their market. Jim was trying to make his living singing commercials in New York. He had a problem because he lived in Connecticut, some ninety miles away. In Jim's line of work, people are often called for work on only a few hours' notice. Although he had a good reputation, potential clients passed Jim by when they saw that he lived so far away. Obviously, if you need somebody to be on the job in two hours, you tend to call someone who lives close by. When we suggested to Jim that he relocate closer to the center of his business, he noted that rents in New York City were much higher than in suburban Connecticut. We pointed out that by living outside the center of his industry, he was undermining his career. Jim was caught up in one of those Catch-22 situations: He couldn't afford to live in New York City. At the same time, he couldn't afford to live outside the area. Our advice to Jim was to find a way to be closer to town, at least during business hours. Jim solved his problem by renting some office space with two other singers in New York and spending most of his time there. Although there were days when he got no calls, he found that business improved steadily. "Basically, it was a case of physically being in New York every day or finding a new line of work," he says now. "The commute from the suburbs is a bit of a drag, but business has picked up to the point that pretty soon I'll be able to afford an apartment in New York."

It's not always absolutely necessary to be in geographic proximity to your clients (though it would be difficult to find an instance where it wouldn't be desirable). A number of successful writers, for example, live outside of major publishing centers and conduct their business through agents who are located in these centers.

No matter what field you're in, it is important to determine the geographical considerations of your particular business and figure out if you are advantageously located to serve a sufficient number of clients.

What are your clients' needs?

Once you know who your clients are and where they are located, you've got to convince them that you are capable of solving their problems. The only way to get hired is to get into the client's orbit and convince him that you can provide something he values. If you're a photographer trying to get work from the art director of a magazine that has just switched to a four-color format, you'd be wasting time for both of you by showing him your portfolio of black-and-white photographs.

Part of what makes you look good to your customers is an

ability to address their particular needs. The more you know about your client and his business, the better you can communicate to that person. Through the sources for information we listed on page 249, you ought to be able to find out all kinds of things about a particular customer. Has he or she just been promoted? Has he been honored for some notable achievement lately? Has his company started a new product line? Has it just had a major cutback in personnel? All of these things are easy to find out once you don your trusty detective cap.

What's going on in the world that affects your business?

Newspapers are one of the best and most overlooked sources of information that can affect your business decisions. Are book publishers going through some hard economic times? If so, this might not be the best time to approach them for work designing book covers. Is there a sudden demand for educational videotapes because more people are taking courses at home? If so, this might be a good time to try to market that learn-at-home computer course you've been designing.

All industries are affected in some way by overall economic and political conditions as well as by specific events that impact a particular field. The energy crisis of the late 1970s, for example, caused an increase in fuel prices, which caused economic difficulties for many businesses. In the record industry, for instance, the rise in fuel costs meant that record prices had to rise at the same time that consumers were already burdened by skyrocketing prices at the supermarket and the gasoline station. Naturally, the record industry suffered at that time. If you were a freelancer servicing that industry, the newspapers might have helped you decide to look for work elsewhere. On the other hand, if your specialty was public relations writing, that might have been a great time to contact the oil companies who were suffering from negative image problems.

Freelancers who keep abreast of current events open themselves up to a wealth of potentially vital information. Not only can they make more informed business decisions, they are better able to speak intelligently with clients about issues that affect them both. The more you know about events that relate to your industry, the better you will be able to communicate your expertise to customers.

What's the competition up to?

Although competition has never deterred successful people in any field, it is a factor that requires careful consideration. Some of your most useful information comes from knowing who your competitors are and what they are doing. The more you know, the easier it is to get a leg up on others in the same line of work. This doesn't mean that you should view your competitors as enemies. Freelancers and consultants in the same field often help each other, particularly when they are not competing head to head. They share contacts, provide reciprocal feedback, and exchange a variety of other information and services. Some people, however, feel so threatened by competition, they become

Researching the competition

totally closed. But others are open and willing to help. They serve as mentors to younger people trying to break into the field and cooperate with their peers whenever they can. People who operate on this kind of reciprocal basis understand that in providing assistance to others, they are ultimately helping themselves.

Contacts:
PEOPLE ARE YOUR MOST IMPORTANT RESOURCE

> You must develop a contact network. It is the most essential, most effective, and least expensive marketing technique available and you cannot succeed without it.
>
> —Jeffrey Lant[5]

People are the most integral component of your marketing program. People hire you; they refer you to others; they give you leads that can turn into assignments; they can make crucial suggestions about how you present yourself. Successful men and women will tell you that they've gotten where they are through the considerable assistance of their contact network. Jack Trout and Al Ries put it this way: "It may be difficult for the ego to accept, but success in life is based more on what others can do for you than on what you can do for yourself."[6] Let's examine this thought a little further. We're not suggesting that competence and self-reliance aren't important, but how far do you think you can get without the help of others? In some cases, you can't even get through to a potential client on the phone without a contact.

Contacts

"It's very rare that I am approached for work by someone who isn't referred by a person I know," says Business Decisions, Inc., marketing consultant Newton Frank, expressing the consensus view of people who regularly employ independent contractors. "I don't get many cold calls from freelancers without an entree of some kind; that type of approach generally doesn't work in many businesses. . . . Most freelancers who have been working for awhile develop a network. That's how they get their work—through that network. From the client's point of view, a referral is kind of an assurance: If you worked for him, you must be competent."

It is an interesting contradiction that while many self-employed people complain about loneliness and isolation, these same people are often uncomfortable about pursuing contacts.

We've often wondered why people who welcome the opportunity to talk on the phone or have lunch with a friend avoid the same kinds of interactions with people who can further their careers. Perhaps they fear that if they attempt to approach business contacts they will be rejected. Some freelancers also seem to think it is improper to call people in order to further their own purposes, that it is somehow wrong to make the first move. "If I ask her to have lunch with me," the reasoning goes, "she'll know that I'm trying to use her." It never occurs to people who reason this way that the world turns on the principle of reciprocation. One hand washes the other may be a crass way of putting it, but that really isn't too far off the mark.

Don't Get Hung Up About "Using" People

There is a song called "Use Me Up" by Bill Withers. This song isn't exactly talking about building contact networks, but the same principle applies. Most of us have grown up believing that "being used" is somehow wrong. In the present context, to "use" someone is to pay them a compliment. It tells them that you recognize their expertise and position and that you value their help. Most successful people have made extensive use of contact networks, so they understand what you are attempting to do. They know it's rough out there and that we all need the help of others to achieve our success. As Adele Scheele puts it:

> The buddy system, based on Connections, allows us to pursue and be pursued by others in our profession without fear and embarrassment. The fact is that we *are* dependent on each other. It's just that simple, and too often we refuse to acknowledge it.[7]

Where to Begin

No matter how little of a conscious effort you've made up till now to develop and expand your contacts, you are probably sitting with all kinds of untapped human resources. Hopefully, you don't have the attitude that all the plums in this world are given to those with friends and relatives in high places. We're not denying that this kind of thing happens, or that your life wouldn't be made easier if you had a well-placed uncle—but consider this: You might have some terrific contacts that you've never bothered to tap. Again, you've got to be something of a detective to ferret them out.

Have you hunted down every clue, followed every lead? We've previously mentioned the concept that you are only three steps away from anyone you want to get in touch with. In other words, someone you knows knows someone who has a friend who can probably get you to the person you are after. Good detectives diligently track down their man (or woman) through this kind of geometric networking. Even if you're new in town or at the early stages of your career, or an introvert with few friends, there are all kinds of things you can do to develop an extensive network of contacts and connections. The question is: Are you going to sit around groaning about what you lack, or are you going to take the cards you're sitting with and parlay them into a winning hand?

Plugging into Contact Networks

Family: This is often your best resource, but one that is easily overlooked just because it is so obvious. Parents and siblings will usually go out of their way to help, or introduce you to anyone they can, but this is only a beginning. Aunts, uncles, cousins, etc., can also be valuable contacts. In our fast-paced, me-oriented society, families aren't as close as they once were. Still, many people feel a unique connection to their relatives and some sense that they would like to be closer. Do you have a cousin who is an attorney? When was the last time you had lunch with him (or her), or updated him about what you were doing?

Pat, a freelance public relations writer, ran into a second cousin who was a corporate executive. After they renewed acquaintances, the cousin revealed that his company recently was seeking someone with Pat's background and skills. "Why didn't you call me?" Pat asked half-jokingly. Her cousin replied, "The last time I saw you, seven years ago, you were teaching school. I had no idea you were a public relations writer." This kind of thing happens all the time. People who would like to do something for you and are in a position to do so have no idea that you need their help. Do yourself a big favor: Keep people apprised of what you are doing so that they can be of service to you. Of all your contact networks, your family may be the one with the strongest motivation to participate in your success.

Business associates: Do you keep in touch with others in your field? Although some of these folks are your direct competitors, they can sometimes be turned into your strongest allies. We know of people in the same line of work who do all sorts of things to help each other. They share materials, discuss each other's portfolios and proposals, and, yes, even share clients. This can be a little touchy at times, but again, the principle of reciprocation applies. If you're a writer of children's books and you've gotten an assignment from an editor who is looking for other authors, wouldn't you turn a friend on to the assignment? We operate on this basis and so do other experienced business people. Someone is going to get that assignment. If it's not going to be you, then why not a friend or someone in your contact network? This is in no way altruism. On the contrary, when you help someone else in this way, you can expect the favor to be returned at some point.

Your network of business associates begins with your peers, yet it is far more extensive than that. As Dr. Jeffrey Lant puts it: "Everyone you have worked with in the past or work with now is a professional associate."[8] Do you let your clients know what you are doing by sending them relevant samples or articles about you that appear in trade journals? Perhaps even more important, do you let them know that you are aware of *their* activities and accomplishments? Advertising executive Al Ries feels that this can be a highly effective way of making clients aware of you:

"One of the easiest and cheapest ways to keep yourself in the minds of buyers is to send them things that pertain to them. If I send something to the head of Burger King that mentions their corporate name, I'm doing it to put *my name* in front of him for a few moments to remind him about me. Sometimes, I might also send something about me to a client. But mostly, they're more interested if their name is in the paper than if your name is in the paper.

When a freelancer sends me a mailing about my company, I appreciate it. It shows that I'm important to him. Then I thank him and I tend to remember his name. . . . During that time that a freelancer's name is in front of me, I might remember that I wanted to talk to him or use him for an upcoming project."

Schools, alumni, and fraternal organizations: It would probably be wise to join as many organizations of this kind as you possibly can. Dues are often relatively modest and the potential for contacts is unlimited. If you attended a major university or belonged to a national fraternity or sorority, you have a potentially valuable contact network to draw upon. Read the publications of these organizations and take note of important people in fields that touch upon your own. Do not hesitate to write or call such people if you feel it can be helpful.

Professional organizations: In many fields, this is a primary source of contacts. Not only does it put you in touch with people and publications that relate to your field, it places you in situations where you can meet people in a social context before presenting your qualifications. Many top editors and literary agents, for example, attend writers' conventions throughout the year. It often happens that you are standing next to an important person without even knowing it when a friendly conversation begins. A few minutes later, when the conversation gets around to asking each other what you do, you've already developed a rapport. At that point, you may find that a highly desirable contact is inviting you to call her or send in your manuscript. This scenario is not uncommon. To the contrary, it happens all the time to people who make it a point to be at places where they can meet professionals who can help them.

Civic and religious groups: Here again, you are narrowing the world down to people with whom you have something in common, be it religious faith or a mutual interest in some issue. When you meet people on this basis, you have the opportunity to gain what Jeffrey Lant calls "automatic acceptance."[9] You aren't there specifically looking for work, so you can get to know people before the topic ever comes up. In many instances, someone will take an interest in what you do because he or she has gotten to know you as a peer on another basis. By the time he discovers that you are looking for the kind of work he is in a position to provide, you've already made a favorable personal impression, and your task is that much easier.

Lectures and courses: If an important person in your field is conducting a course or giving a lecture, try to attend if you possibly can. Don't feel shy about approaching the person and trying to establish a relationship. Many freelancers have found mentors and other contacts in these settings. Even if you can't have an extensive conversation with the person while the lecture or course is going on, ask for an address so that you can make contact at a later date. Some successful people are more open and helpful than others. Don't get discouraged if you are rebuffed by a contact you're attempting to pursue. Remember: There is no such thing as a perfect batting average in anything. As you develop more experience in connecting with others, you will become more sensitive to the messages you are giving and receiving. Perhaps the person doesn't like something about the way you are presenting yourself, or perhaps he is distracted by a personal matter or some pressing business just when you approach him. As time goes by, you will become more adept at reading people's signals. But you must utilize opportunities to connect with others as they come your way. Lectures and courses are good training grounds because they allow you to interact informally not only with the lecturer, but with the other people in attendance.

Guidelines for Connecting

Connecting is more of an art than a science. There aren't very many hard or fast rules for how to do it. We suggest that you start reaching out in as many of the directions we've discussed as you can to develop and expand your network of contacts. There is really no better schooling than the experience you'll get from immersing yourself in the almost infinite network of contacts that is available to anyone who wants to plug into it. Don't get discouraged if you feel uncomfortable at first. Connecting will become a habit that can help you in anything you attempt in life. With practice, you will find your own style and become comfortable reaching out to people. Here are a few basic guidelines to assist you along the way:

Keep a record of all your contacts

If you are going to launch the kind of ongoing connecting program we are endorsing, there is no way to keep all the names and relevant information in your head. We suggest that you start a comprehensive record-keeping system of all your contacts. There are a number of ways to go about this. One of the most common is a file of three-by-five-inch cards on which you keep any and all pertinent information about each of your contacts. This might include:

- Name, address, telephone number, exact title

- Name of the person who referred you

- Names of all contacts stemming from this person

- Any personal information that might help you communicate better

- Dates when you communicated; nature of those communications

- Follow-up—which should also be recorded in your appointment book

Does all of this seem like a lot of tedious and unnecessary work? Once you recognize the importance of contact networks and make the habit of utilizing them as a part of your routine, you'll find that it only takes a minute to pull the pertinent file card and record the necessary information. You may also feel that a good portion of this work will never pay off in an actual assignment. But how do you know up front which contacts will pay off? There is a popular concept called the "80/20 rule," which maintains that you get 80 percent of your results from 20 percent of your resources. This means that most of your work will come from a relatively small percentage of your contacts. Since you really have no way of predicting who this 20 percent will be, you have to begin with the assumption that all your contacts are important and work from there.

Whenever possible, socialize with your contacts

If you can get an important contact to have lunch with you or have drinks after work, you may be opening doors that would otherwise be closed to you. We've noticed that many highly successful people completely integrate their business and social lives. The same colleague they are concluding a major deal with on Friday afternoon can often be found breaking bread at Saturday dinner. Some freelancers aren't comfortable mixing business with pleasure and they prefer to separate the two as much as possible. Career coach Adele Scheele feels that this type of attitude tends to limit one's potential:

> *Business is pleasure.* It is a mistake to think that there's anything but a mix. . . . People who answer ads in the paper or use [similar] . . . systems are very different people from those who use personal networks. The ones who use the networks are much the stronger, for they demonstrate their willingness to take chances and to participate in a positive human system. . . . [This kind of] participation works best if you invest wholeheartedly in the process. You need to appreciate other people's time. You need to care about their work. You need to value people's stories and experiences, for they are the stuff of life itself, and can lead you to some of your own most rewarding experiences.[10]

Be a good listener

It's a mistake to think that you have to be an aggressive talker to utilize contacts effectively. On the contrary, the most important thing you can do is listen. When you call someone up or go to see them in person, give them an opportunity to talk about *their* business, *their* personal life, *their* upcoming vacation. The more the other person talks, the better it is for you. Everyone likes people who are interested in what they are saying, and that certainly includes your contacts. Also, when you give someone else a chance to talk, you are likely to find out information that can be important to you. When you walk into someone's office and say, "Tell me about your new division," you've done several positive things: You've indicated that you are interested and knowledgeable about that individual's company; you've also given him or her the chance to tell you something that might affect your presentation; and you've opened the door for a more cordial interaction.

Remember your implicit obligation to those who help you

The principle of reciprocation is the foundation of mutually beneficial contacts. You will find that people will sometimes help you even though they don't really want anything in return. Still, at the very least, we owe something to those who further our career, even if it's just a phone call and a periodic updating of our progress. People who plug into contact networks don't generally operate on a tit-for-tat basis. They realize that somewhere down the road their helpfulness is likely to pay off in a variety of ways. From the point of view of the person receiving the help, we urge you to make it a point to do the following whenever someone goes out of their way to help you:

✔ Send a thank-you note and/or call.

✔ If something positive comes from their suggestion, let them know.

✔ Consider sending a modest gift or taking to lunch someone who has gone out of their way on your behalf.

✔ If you come across an opportunity to do something for that person, do so without being asked.

Pricing and Terms:
WHAT YOU GET FOR
WHAT YOU GIVE

LET'S ASSUME FOR THE MOMENT THAT YOU'RE highly motivated, well-structured, and have an extensive network of contacts. Your phone is ringing off the hook from clients calling with work. Inevitably, they ask the one question that throws you: "How much will it cost?"

One of our favorite examples of the problems in setting an appropriate price comes from a scene in a movie about the advertising business called *Putney Swope*. A young photographer named Mark Focus walks up to ad agency president Putney Swope with his portfolio. The following conversation takes place:

MF: Mr. Swope, Mark Focus. (Showing samples from his portfolio) I did that for Hertz, that's Colgate, that's Nabisco. . . .

PS: I've seen enough, Mark. You're one of the best photographers in the business.

MF: Thank you.

PS: This print ad I'm working on is perfect for you.

MF: If it's me, it's nine thousand.

PS: Nine thousand! I just want a picture of a light bulb with lipstick on it.

MF: Make it six.

PS: Hey, man, it's going in a newspaper, not an art gallery.

MF: Twelve hundred is the best I can do.

        (PS gazes noncommitally and says nothing)

MF: Three-fifty.

        (PS glares at him and says nothing)

MF: (Plaintively) I'll do it for nothing. I need the work!

PS: I can get anybody for nothing. Take a walk!

        (MF walks away in a huff)

We understand that this is an extreme example in the context of a rather absurd film. Yet this little snippet of conversation gets right to the heart of the kinds of problems freelancers have in pricing their work. The most frequent dilemma is finding some kind of happy medium between your desire to get as much money as you can and your anxiety about losing the job by asking for too much. What to do?

Ask around: Pricing is a vital part of your market research. Before you discuss terms with a client, find out how much people are getting for similar assignments. Here are a few suggestions for obtaining this kind of information:

◗ Ask your contacts in the industry what the going rate is.

◗ Find out if any unions, guilds, or professional associations have minimum or standard prices. Ask attorneys, reps, and other experts in your field.

◗ Look for clues in trade papers.

◗ Find out what that client normally pays.

◗ Consult the Department of Labor's Bureau of Statistics.

We find that freelancers often err on the low rather than the high side of the pricing spectrum. That is, they ask too little for their work because they are afraid that they will lose the assignment if they ask what they consider an appropriate price. Furthermore, we come across many freelancers who don't even figure out what they need to make the assignment worthwhile.

If you think of yourself as a business, one of your implicit goals is financial profit. Since you are an entrepreneur, you are entitled to something more than a per-hour fee for your labor. If you subcontracted the work to another freelancer, he or she would only receive an hourly wage. As a going business, you deserve to be paid for all the time and effort you put into getting the work. Just remember: Profit is the energy source for the growth of your business.[11] Make sure you build it into your price.

We're well aware that people often accept jobs that pay less than the price they would like to charge. Nevertheless, we think it's important to know what your price is. If you decide to accept the assignment for a lower price, you ought to know why. Perhaps that job will bring you publicity and open the door for more work, perhaps it is something you always wanted to do, or perhaps you want to get in the good graces of a potentially important client. In any case, you shouldn't accept a job just because it is offered. We know this can be difficult at times, but we feel strongly that if a job isn't fulfilling some of your objectives, it is better to turn it down.

A Brief Course in Negotiating

Some people who work for themselves choose to negotiate through lawyers and agents. In many industries, that is definitely the way to go. However, there are times when you may have to negotiate for yourself and come to terms with a client. Here are some things to consider in such situations:

Start high, not low: "A good negotiator tries to secure for himself all the advantages of a deal without blowing that deal," says Seymour Feig, a highly respected entertainment attorney who is an adjunct professor of entertainment law and negotiation at New York Law School. "As a rule, when you're talking price, you start on the highest rung that you can. Then, if you have to come down in your price, you can try to make it up on your other terms."

One problem independent contractors have in setting price—particularly in the early stages of their careers—is that they are afraid that the client will say "Forget it" if they ask for a reasonable, never mind a high, price. They are so afraid of losing the assignment they accept a price that undermines their objectives.

"A lot of people accept a bad price, hoping to establish credibility with the user," notes Feig. "That rarely works. The user tends to think less of you. Far from appreciating the good turn you've done him, he goes elsewhere the next time. I find that more times than not, bottom-dollar chargers only get called for bottom-dollar assignments. When the client has a higher-paying assignment, he will go elsewhere."

Let's pretend you are trying to come to terms with a client. You've started off with a high-end price that he says he simply can't meet. In some instances, the best thing you can do is tell him you'll think about it and inevitably turn down the job. On the other hand, dollars might not be the only important thing to you. Before you walk into the meeting, you should know every other thing you can ask for that might offset a lower price. These may include:

◊ The prominent appearance of your name on the work and all publicity for the work

◊ Finished samples of the work

◊ An allowance for expenses and supplies

◊ A larger portion of the fee up front

◊ Greater creative freedom

◊ Subsidiary rights

Any of these terms can potentially offset a lower price if you handle them correctly. Subsidiary rights, in industries where they apply, can be particularly lucrative. For example, the author of a book may accept a lower advance in exchange for a higher percentage of magazine or foreign reprint rights. A cartoonist can license the right to a character for use in a comic strip and maintain all other rights to the character, such as tee shirts, dolls, and other merchandising items. In most cases, subsidiary rights issues require the expertise of a lawyer, agent, or other expert in that particular field. But you owe it to yourself to be well apprised of any and all terms that can benefit you.

Don't price yourself out of the ballpark. Since negotiating is a complex and subtle form of communication, it is vital that freelancers understand the process from the client's point of view as well as their own. While he doesn't disagree that freelancers tend to undervalue their services, advertising executive Al Ries has run into individuals who ask what he considers outrageous fees for their work. He suggests that this practice will not only lose you the job, but the chance to get assignments in the future:

"My experience is that when a client asks for a price, make sure you quote a price that's reasonable. It's better to turn down a job than to quote an unreasonable price. If you were paving your driveway and one guy quotes you a $5,000 price and a second guy quotes you a $10,000 price, would you ever use that second guy again? I know I wouldn't.

"There could be lots of reasons why his price was so

high. Maybe he was so busy at the time he would have needed to subcontract the work. Maybe he's even losing money charging $10,000. Better not to take the job than to quote an unreasonable price. I'm not saying you shouldn't go for a high price. I'm saying don't charge a price that's out of line. One way freelancers stay busy is by establishing price dependability. When I get to know someone I sometimes give out work without even discussing price because I know it will be in the ballpark."

Learn to read body language and other subtle cues. What does the client do when you quote your price? Does he smile or does he look like he's going to fall out of his chair? Any experienced negotiator will tell you that the messages the other person sends are vital signals in any negotiation. "I never negotiate an important deal over the phone," says Seymour Feig. "To me the art of negotiation involves eye contact, facial expression, and body movement. After you've been doing it for a while, you can tell by the glint in a person's eye, the movement of their chin, and other gestures if you're in the ballpark or if they're thinking of what you say adversely."

Experienced negotiators quickly get a feel for the person they are dealing with. They sense nervousness and tension and learn how to use these to their best advantage. Because freelancers often don't have as much negotiating experience as their clients, they can sometimes be fooled by intentionally misleading body language or overpowered by a more polished negotiator's confident style. That doesn't mean you are defeated before you even begin. Remember, you always have some power when you negotiate. After all, the client wouldn't even be talking to you at this point if you didn't have something he or she needs. Try to make the most of your own personal style and life experiences when you negotiate. Don't try to outtalk a fast talker if you are laid back by nature. Ideally, negotiations should be win-win rather than win-lose situations. Try to project a positive attitude that says you are looking for solutions that will satisfy everyone involved.

Speak to the person in power. If often happens that after talking terms with someone for hours, you find out that he doesn't have the power to make the deal. Whenever possible, try to talk to the person who is doing the hiring rather than a subordinate. Organizational protocol and other factors sometimes make this difficult. At the very least, know the position of the person you are dealing with. If possible, try to get to someone on a higher organizational rung. Otherwise, you can waste time or have your messages misinterpreted to the person who makes the final decision.

Consider your client's point of view. Always remember that although clients need freelancers, they ultimately decide which ones they are going to hire. It is only natural for freelancers to be more concerned with their own considerations than with those that affect their clients. By the same token, you can expect your customers to be more attached to their side of the picture than to yours. In order to market yourself effectively, you will benefit if you know as much as you can about the client's side of the coin. Here's what advertising exec and author Al Ries has to say on this subject:

"Freelancers tend to be me-oriented. They often don't recognize or even consider the needs of the client. Since buyers ultimately decide whether or not freelancers get the business, their opinion is really the most important part of the whole equation. It's like the old saying: 'The customer is always right.'

"When you discuss price with the buyer, don't only consider the fee you set for your work. Find out what he's going to use that work for and what his budget is for the entire job. . . . If you're an artist who's called by G.E. to do a piece of artwork for a four-color annual report, you know the budget is probably $1 million and you can set your price accordingly. On the other hand, G.E. might ask for a piece of artwork for a sales meeting. If you don't know what the buyer wants to use the work for, you might not understand that difference in price."

Try not to give your final answer on the spot. After all the talking is done and some kind of understanding is in the wind, you would be wise to say something like: "Sounds good; let me get back to you." There are several reasons for postponing your final decision. As you can see, negotiations are often complex affairs. Since you may not be the world's most experienced negotiator, you might reconsider one or more points after you've had a little time to think about it. Also, you send a message to the client that you aren't hungry or chomping at the bit to get the assignment. This kind of attitude makes you look more professional in the client's eyes.

In considering any offer, you might want to call your lawyer or some other expert to make certain you haven't left anything out or compromised your position. If there is a problem, you can call the client and bring it to his attention. If you decide that you want to undertake the assignment, call the client and reiterate the terms you agreed on. By calling the client and initiating the interaction, you are giving yourself the advantage of being more prepared. This approach is far better than making a deal in haste, before you've had some time to think it over. Also—be suspicious of any client who says you've got to let him know on the spot. Barring some unusual situation, most reputable business people respect your desire to consider your position away from the heat and pressure of the actual negotiation.

When you reach an agreement, put it in writing. Counsels Seymour Feig:

"Every job, no matter how small, should have a written agreement. Otherwise, you have nothing to hang your hat on if you have to take the person to court. There ought to be a writing that covers every single service or material you are issuing to a user. All you need is a simple letter saying you hired me to do such and such at this price and with these stipulations. That is a legal document as long as the client signs the letter and acknowledges the terms. People sometimes think it's enough to send a letter stating the terms without asking the client for a written acknowledgment. These are just self-serving declarations that mean nothing in court."

Here is a sample letter that might cover a simple assignment. More complex contracts should be examined by an attorney or other expert:

John Jones Artist   #60723
140 West Avenue
New York, N.Y.

Agreement made this day _____ between John Jones Artist and XYZ Co. Jones agrees to deliver to XYZ Co. a finished oil painting ($48'' \times 48''$) (to be reproduced in their year-end report) within 60 days. The full agreed upon price for this painting is $1,500. Terms $500 in advance, $500 upon approval of sketch, and the balance of $500 to be paid within 2 weeks of delivery and acceptance of finished painting. Major last minute changes decided upon by XYZ Co. after approval of sketch to be billed at $150 per day's work (6 hours).

_____

John Jones

_____

XYZ Co.

Freelancers sometimes feel that their relationship with a client is so strong that a simple handshake will suffice. This can lead to misunderstandings and bad feelings on everyone's part. With the passage of time, people tend to remember things quite differently from the way they were originally said, usually from their own vantage point. Don't take the attitude that asking for a written agreement is an unfriendly thing to do. In fact, written contracts help maintain friendships. If the contract is a simple letter of agreement, try to draw it up yourself instead of asking the client to send it to you. There are always slight differences in the way terms are worded that tend to favor the party that draws up the agreement.

Billing. Once you've delivered an assignment and it has been accepted by the client, the next step is getting paid. Are you aware of the billing procedures in your industry? In many businesses, the person who you deliver the work to has nothing to do with sending your check out. Find out if you have to send an invoice in order to get paid. Also, it might be a good idea to specify how long after delivery you can expect payment. Once you've had experience with a client, you tend to rely on his good faith, but people have gotten stiffed on occasion. Even major corporations may delay payment.

Imagine this scenario from the point of view of a large corporation. The going money market rate is 15 percent (which it was several times in the last few years), and you are sitting with $1 million in unpaid bills. If you hold on to that money for an additional thirty days, you can pick up a nice piece of change in interest ($12,500.). What we're saying is this: For a variety of reasons, people and companies hate to let go of cash. At times, it may become necessary for you to remind the client that you delivered your part of the agreement and now you expect to be paid. After all the effort you've put into the project, you wouldn't want to neglect this rather important phase.

TAKING IT TO THE STREET

ARE YOU GETTING THE RESULTS YOU WANT FROM your current marketing efforts? If not, why not? The answer probably lies in the way you've been operating. We may not think about it in these terms, but everybody utilizes some kind of Operating Procedure. We all expend a certain amount of energy looking for work, and we all reap some kind of results. The question is: What kind of results are you getting relative to your efforts? People who don't put much energy into the kinds of things we've been discussing in this chapter shouldn't be mystified if business is slow. If, on the other hand, you've been trying hard but still can't seem to pull it all together, you need to play detective again and figure out which piece of the puzzle is missing. Let's briefly review the components of the kind of ongoing marketing program we've been discussing:

O Self-presentation—How do you and your materials look to others?

O Marketing research—How much do you know about your business?

O Contacts—How well do you utilize the vast network of human resources?

O Pricing—How do the prices you charge affect your ability to get work?

Is there something about the way you are handling one of these areas that is preventing an otherwise sound marketing program from getting off the ground? Here are three examples of freelancers who managed to pinpoint their problems:

"You're really good, but . . . ." Jill is a talented writer who recently moved to New York from Chicago. Although she didn't know many people in her new city, Jill did what she could to make contacts. She found out about a Wednesday afternoon writers' lunch and attended it regularly. She joined professional organizations and took classes with teachers who might be in a position to help her. Jill had done "a little bit of everything," as she put it, in Chicago. She wrote a few magazine articles, a children's book, some advertising copy, and a smattering of press releases. Since she was new in town, she was eager to get any kind of work she could. It seemed only logical to look through her previous work and put together a portfolio of what she considered to be her best writings.

After a year in New York, Jill had only received a few very low-paying assignments, and was baffled by her poor results. She had been to see a number of editors, most of whom responded favorably to her work. Still, the jobs were few and far between. One day Jill was speaking with an editor she felt comfortable with. After the editor praised her work, Jill asked her straight out if she thought there would be a paying assignment any time soon. When the editor hedged, Jill said: "I would really appreciate your feedback. Is there something about my work that is preventing you from hiring me?"

"You're a very talented writer," the editor replied. "But I'm not sure how I can use you."

From our vantage point, Jill's presentation was much too general. By not focusing in on one writing skill, she didn't position herself in a way potential clients could relate to. We suggested that Jill make a separate writing sample package for each of her specialties and present the one that was most likely to meet the needs of each client she went to see.

"I never know when you're out there. . . ." Frank is a graphic designer who noticed that he was getting less work from his regular clients over an eighteen-month period. He couldn't pinpoint his problem. He had a very good reputation in his field for delivering quality work at a fair price. Friends with fewer

credentials were getting more work than they could handle, but Frank wasn't getting enough. We suggested to Frank that he survey his friends and find out everything they were doing to get work. He found that the ones who were really busy kept in touch with their clients regularly, both by phone and personal contact. Frank refused to believe that this was the source of his problem. After all, some of his clients had been calling him for years. "They know where to reach me if they need me," he reasoned. We encouraged Frank to approach one of his long-standing clients directly and ask why more work wasn't forthcoming. Frank took our advice and reported the following conversation:

FRANK: I was wondering why you haven't been calling me on a more regular basis. Is there any problem with my work?

CLIENT: Not at all. I've always been well pleased with your work and I really would like to use you more.

FRANK: How come you don't then? Is there less work now than there used to be?

CLIENT: No. The work is still there. It's just that the people I use regularly call me all the time to let me know that they're available. Sometimes I don't hear from you for months, and I assume that you're just not interested. I never know when you're out there because you don't keep in touch that often.

Frank realized that he has to keep his clients apprised of his desire to work. "I just assumed that after a while they'd automatically call me when something came up. How wrong I was!"

Targeting the wrong customers . . . Donna had turned her basement into a word-processing center after investing thousands of dollars in the latest equipment. She believed that the many students and writers who lived in her neighborhood would provide a steady stream of term papers and manuscripts as a foundation for her enterprise. Donna was very optimistic about her chances for success. There were no other word-processing centers in her area. Also, because she would be operating out of her home, Donna would be able to keep her prices low and still make a profit. Three months after she opened her doors, however, the flow of customers was, as she put it, "almost nonexistent."

At this point, Donna surveyed some local writers and students, and quickly got to the root of her problem. Most of Donna's potential customers were getting their work typed by freelancers in the neighborhood for $.80 a page. Donna's price of $4.00 a page was reasonable for word processing. Unfortunately, most of the clients she was trying to reach didn't require storage of information on a disk, variable lettering styles, and other advantages word processors provide—not at five times the price.

As we see it, Donna made one crucial omission in her market research. She didn't find out who her real competitors were and what they were offering. Had she spoken to potential customers beforehand, she would have realized that her service did not provide enough added value to offset the substantial difference in price. Donna has started retargeting her service to address the needs of small businesses in her community who can better utilize the advantages of word processing.

How Do You Stack Up Against the Competition?

No matter what business you're in, chances are there are people—quite often lots of people—who are trying to do the same kind of work. That's why it's not enough to market yourself well. Somehow, you've got to find a way to market yourself better than the people you are up against. There are a number of ways to go about this while still maintaining your sense of ethics and personal integrity, but you've got to start by accepting the fact that it's a crowded world out there, so you've got to come up with a way of making yourself stand out from the crowd. We strongly suggest that you evaluate your marketing efforts in the light of the following questions:

SIX THINGS EVERY FREELANCER SHOULD KNOW ABOUT THE COMPETITION

1. Who are your competitors?

2. What are they doing that you can learn from?

3. What can you do that they're not doing?

4. What are they charging?

5. What are their strengths?

6. What are their weaknesses?

Strategy and competitive positioning

Once you can answer these questions about the competition, you can figure out how to get a leg up on them. We've discussed the importance of positioning—i.e., the ability to get a clear and concise message to potential customers. But good communication is only the first step. After you succeed at letting someone know what you do, you've got to convince that person to hire you. Put yourself in your client's shoes and ask yourself this: What is it about my work that gives me an advantage over the next guy? Here are some possibilities:

WHY I'M GOING TO GET THE JOB

☞   I produce better quality work than my competitors.

☞   I deliver work faster than my competitors.

☞   I charge less than my competitors.

☞   I utilize my contacts better than my competitors.

☞   I've got a better track record than my competitors.

☞   Other.

If you can pinpoint your strengths in one or more of these areas, you can develop a strategy from there. In some cases, your competitive advantage may rest in the image you project rather than some tangible aspect of your work.

Let's look at another example from the world of advertising. Avis was losing money for years until it *positioned* itself as the car rental company that tries harder. Whether they actually do "try harder" than Hertz never has been established, yet the public recognizes Avis by these three words: *We try harder*. There are many other companies that have built their success on image rather than on any real differences. Is there something you can do to make yourself stand out in the mind of your client? Maybe you can be like Avis and position yourself as the cabinetmaker who puts more care into his or her craft, or maybe you can develop a reputation as the financial advisor who takes a personal interest in his or her clients. Whether you are stressing a real or perceived value in your attempts to attract customers, success in today's competitive marketplace requires a well-thought-out strategy.

Here are some questions that can help you develop a marketing strategy that works for you:

1. Are you aware of what's going on in your industry at this time?

2. Do you know what your competitors are doing to get work?

3. Have you evaluated yourself in terms of the major components of an ongoing market program?

4. Do you know where your strengths and weaknesses lie?

5. What would you say your strongest point is in the mind of your clients?

6. Have you been considering your competitor's strengths and weaknesses relative to your own?

7. If you've been utilizing a strategy, write two sentences stating what it is based on.

8. What one area of your marketing program could you focus on to improve your results?

9. Are you aware of any additional information you could obtain that might help you formulate a better marketing strategy?

10. Is there anything in your personal style that can enhance your strategy?

Minimize Your Weaknesses and Maximize Your Strengths

Take a survey of the top people in any field. Do they possess every single possible quality a person in their position could have? Probably not. The best tennis players always have some weaknesses in their game, just as the greatest musicians generally have some area in which they do not excel. We find that people who succeed are those who learn to emphasize their strengths and work around their weaknesses. As we've seen, there are a number of relatively complex and interacting processes that go into an effective marketing program, but that doesn't mean you've got to do them all equally well or attack them all at once.

We suggest that you shore up those areas in which you are deficient. If your portfolio stinks, concentrate on improving it. If you've been avoiding personal contact with people who can help you, start getting in touch. In other words, plug up any gaping holes.

At the same time, you need to begin to emphasize those things that you're strongest in. If you are uncomfortable talking to people on the phone, but adept at writing letters and proposals, build your plan of action around that strength. Once you take an honest look at your strong and weak points, you can save time, effort, and aggravation by accentuating the positive and minimizing the negative. Let's take a case in point.

Go with your own personal style

Bill is a financial consultant who always had what he called a "shyness problem." Though he was skilled at his work, he always felt that he would never succeed because clients would look askance at his lack of aggressiveness. We suggested that he write his sales talk down on three-by-five-inch cards and keep them handy at initial meetings with customers. We also urged him to emphasize his ability to listen well—an attribute that is often far more valuable than the gift of gab. Like anyone in any business, Bill won some and lost some, but more often than not, people responded to his personal style. A few potential clients may have been more comfortable with an aggressive talker, but the ones who chose to work with Bill saw in him the following qualities:

$ He listens well and understands what I'm saying.

$ When he does speak, he gets his ideas across effectively.

$ He is prepared and asks relevant questions about my needs.

$ He seems comfortable in his dealings and this conveys an air of competence.

People who lead with their strengths understand that they may not achieve their objective each time out. Since you're not going to bat 1.000 no matter what you do, it makes sense to go with the personal style that is most comfortable for you. Remember, our overriding purpose in this book is to help you develop the kind of business and lifestyle you want. The best way to do this is to know as much as you can about yourself and the world around you and put it all together. People who proceed on the basis of some preconceived notion of how things are supposed to get done, without considering their own parameters as human beings, can become very frustrated and never reach their potential.

Epilogue

If you've done some of what we suggest in this book, you've got a lot more information and a sounder basis for action than ever before. We realize that there is a lot of work here for anyone who attempts to utilize the principles we've been discussing. Don't be overwhelmed! If you can begin by plugging up one or two gaping holes, while at the same time building on a few of your obvious strengths, you'll find that things which might seem awkward and difficult at first gradually become easier to work into your daily life. As they start bringing you the kind of results you're after, you'll find that they become a part of you. **Trust your process.**

Footnotes

Chapter Two

1. Robert Moskowitz, *How to Organize Your Work and Your Life* (Garden City, New York: A Dolphin Book/Doubleday & Co., 1981), p. 137.

Chapter Three

1. John Kenneth Galbraith and Nicole Salinger, *Almost Everyone's Guide to Economics* (New York: Bantam Books, 1978), p. 73.
2. Daniel Yankelovich, *New Rules—Searching for Self-Fulfillment in a World Turned Upside Down* (New York: Bantam Books, 1981), p. 53.
3. Jack and Lois Johnstad, *The Power of Prosperous Thinking* (New York: St. Martin's Press, 1982), p. xvi.
4. George S. Clason, *The Richest Man in Babylon* (New York: Bantam Books, 1955), p. 30.
5. Leonard Silk, *Economics in Plain English—All You Need to Know About Economics—In Language Anyone Can Understand* (New York: A Touchstone Book/Simon and Schuster, 1978), p. 57.
6. Dolly Parton, *Parade* Magazine article, "I'm Not Going I'm Just Growing," by Marguerite Michaels, November 2, 1980.
7. Richard K. Rifenbark with David Johnson, *How to Beat the Salary Trap* (New York: Avon Books, 1978), p. 59.

8. William J. Grace, Jr., *The ABC's of IRA's* (New York: Dell Publishing Co., 1982), p. 105.
9. Bonnie Siverd, "Your Financial Team," *Working Woman* Magazine, November 1982.
10. Andrew Tobias, *The Only Investment Guide You'll Ever Need* (New York: Bantam Books, 1978), p. 107.
11. John D. McDonald, *Bright Orange for the Shroud* (Greenwich, Conn.: A Fawcett Gold Medal Book, 1965), p. 5.
12. Rifenbark, *How to Beat the Salary Trap,* p. 67.
13. Clason, *The Richest Man In Babylon,* p. 40.
14. Tobias, *The Only Investment Guide You'll Ever Need,* p. 59.
15. Life Tables for The United States, (Dept. of Health and Human Services, September 1982). (These figures apply to people who will be 65 in the year 2000.)
16. Tobias, *The Only Investment Guide You'll Ever Need,* p. 23.

Chapter Four

1. Og Mandino, *The Greatest Salesman in the World* (New York: Bantam Books, 1968), p. 64.
2. Rollo May, *The Courage to Create* (New York: Bantam Books, 1975), pp. 13–14.
3. Richard Trubo, "Peak Performance," an article about a study by mathematician-psychologist Charles A. Garfield, *Success* Magazine, April 1983, p. 32.
4. Ibid.

Chapter Five

1. Og Mandino, *The Greatest Salesman in the World* (New York: Bantam Books, 1968), p. 54.
2. Miyamoto Musashi, *The Book of Five Rings—The Real Art of Japanese Management* (New York: Bantam Books, 1982) pp. xv–xxxi
3. Rita Davenport, *Making Time, Making Money* (New York: St. Martin's Press, 1982), p. 153.
4. Abraham Maslow, *The Farther Reaches of Human Nature* (New York: Penguin Books, 1971), p. 45.

5. Dru Scott, Ph.D., *How to Put More Time in Your Life* (New York: Rawson, Wade Publishers, 1980), p. 27.

Chapter Six

1. Abraham Maslow, *The Farther Reaches of Human Nature* (New York: Penguin Books, 1971), p. 63.
2. P. T. Barnum, "How to Become a Money Getter" excerpted from Og Mandino, *University of Success* (New York: Bantam Books, 1982), pp. 263–64.
3. Joe Hyams, *Zen in the Martial Arts* (New York: Bantam Books, 1979), p. 39. (Bruce Lee talking)
4. Alan Lakein, *How to Get Control of Your Time and Your Life* (New York: New American Library, 1973), p. 105.
5. Michael LeBoeuf, *The Productivity Challenge—How to Make It Work for America and You* (New York: McGraw-Hill, 1982), p. 212.
6. Stephanie Winston, *Getting Organized—The Easy Way to Put Your Life in Order* (New York: Warner Books, 1979), p. 66.
7. LeBoeuf, *The Productivity Challenge,* p. 188.

Chapter Seven

1. Robert Sam Anson, "David Geffen Talks a Little," *Esquire* Magazine, Nov., 1982.
2. Adele Scheele, Ph.D., *Skills for Success* (New York: Ballantine Books, 1979), p. 12.
3. Ibid., p. 10.
4. Al Ries and Jack Trout, *Positioning—The Battle for Your Mind* (New York: McGraw-Hill, 1981), p. 15.
5. Jeffrey L. Lant, *The Consultants' Kit* (Cambridge, Mass.: JLA Publications, 1981), p. 23.
6. Ries and Trout, *Positioning,* p. 208.
7. Scheele, *Skills for Success,* p. 17.
8. Lant, *The Consultant's Kit,* p. 25.
9. Ibid., p. 24.
10. Scheele, *Skills for Success,* pp. 59–60.
11. Based on a concept from Kenichi Ohmae, *The Mind of the Strategist* (New York: Penguin Books, 1982), p. 29.

Suggested Reading

Chapter Two
THE INDIVIDUAL BUSINESS STRUCTURE (IBS) OR HOW TO RUN THE MOST IMPORTANT BUSINESS ON THIS PLANET . . . YOURS!!!

Thomas J. Peters and Robert H. Waterman, Jr. *In Search of Excellence—Lessons from America's Best-Run Companies*. New York: Harper & Row, 1982.

Leon Tec, M.D. *Targets: How to Set Goals for Yourself and Reach Them*. New York: New American Library, 1980.

William G. Ouchi. *Theory Z—How American Business Can Meet the Japanese Challenge*. New York: Avon Books, 1981.

H. Ronald Kibel. *How to Turn Around a Financially Troubled Company*. New York: McGraw-Hill, 1982.

Chapter Three
GAINING FINANCIAL CONTROL: DEALING WITH MONEY CAN BE A PAIN . . . BUT NOT HAVING IT IS WORSE

Janice Rotchstein. *The Money Diet—How to Save Up to $360 in 28 Days*. New York: Crown Publishers, 1982.

Jerry Gillies. *Moneylove—How to Get the Money You Deserve for Whatever You Want*. New York: Warner Books, 1978.

Richard K. Rifenbark with David Johnson. *How to Beat the Salary Trap*. New York: Avon Books, 1978.

John Kenneth Galbraith and Nicole Salinger. *Almost Everyone's Guide to Economics*. New York: Bantam Books, 1978.

George S. Clason. *The Richest Man in Babylon*. New York: Bantam Books, 1955.

Andrew Tobias. *The Only Investment Guide You'll Ever Need.* New York: Bantam Books, 1978.

Leonard Silk. *Economics in Plain English—All You Need to Know About Economics—In Language Anyone Can Understand.* New York: A Touchstone Book/Simon and Schuster, 1978.

Jack and Lois Johnstad. *The Power of Prosperous Thinking.* New York: St. Martin's Press, 1982.

Michael Phillips. *The Seven Laws of Money.* Menlo Park, Calif. and New York: Word Wheel and Random House, 1974.

Bernard Meltzer. *Bernard Meltzer Solves Your Money Problems.* New York: Simon and Schuster, 1982.

Chapter Four
SUCCESS: WHAT YOU WANT AND HOW TO GET IT

Bernard Gittelson. *How to Make Your Own Luck.* New York: Warner Books, 1981.

Napoleon Hill. *Grow Rich!—With Peace of Mind.* New York: Fawcett Crest, 1967.

Napoleon Hill. *The Master-Key to Riches.* New York: Fawcett Crest, 1965.

Martha Friedman. *Overcoming the Fear of Success.* New York: Warner Books, 1980.

Rollo May, *The Courage to Create.* New York: Bantam Books, 1975.

Abraham H. Maslow. *The Farther Reaches of Human Nature.* New York: Penguin Books, 1971.

Napoleon Hill. *Think and Grow Rich.* New York: Fawcett Crest, 1960.

Daniel Yankelovich. *New Rules—Searching for Self-Fulfillment in a World Turned Upside Down.* New York: Bantam Books, 1981.

Og Mandino. *The Greatest Salesman in the World.* New York: Bantam Books, 1968.

Adele Scheele, Ph.D. *Skills for Success.* New York: Ballantine, 1979.

Philip Slater. *Wealth Addiction.* New York: E. P. Dutton, 1980.

Geoffrey Bailey. *Maverick.* New York: Franklin Watts, 1982.

Chapter Five
HABITS: THE MECHANICS OF DOING

Benjamin Franklin. *The Autobiography and Other Writings*, selected and edited with an Introduction by L. Jesse Lemisch. New York: New American Library, 1961.

Miyamoto Musashi. *The Book of Five Rings—The Real Art of Japanese Management*. New York: Bantam Books, 1982.

Joe Hyams. *Zen in the Martial Arts*. New York: Bantam Books, 1979.

Janwillem van de Wetering. *The Empty Mirror—Experiences in a Japanese Zen Monastery*. New York: Washington Square Press, 1973.

Janwillem van de Wetering. *A Glimpse of Nothingness—Experiences in an American Zen Community*. New York: Washington Square Press, 1975.

Colette Dowling. *The Cinderella Complex*. New York: Pocket Books, 1981.

Chapter Six
TIME: MAKING THE BEST USE OF LIFE'S CURRENCY

Stephanie Winston. *Getting Organized—The Easy Way to Put Your Life in Order*. New York: Warner Books, 1978.

Michael LeBoeuf. *Working Smart—How to Accomplish More in Half the Time*. New York: Warner Books, 1979.

Dru Scott, Ph.D. *How to Put More Time in Your Life*. New York: Rawson, Wade Publishers, 1980.

Alan Lakein. *How to Get Control of Your Time and Your Life*. New York: New American Library, 1973.

Robert Moskowitz. *How to Organize Your Work and Your Life*. Garden City, New York: A Dolphin Book/Doubleday and Co., 1981.

Rita Davenport. *Making Time, Making Money*. New York: St. Martin's Press, 1982.

Michael LeBoeuf. *The Productivity Challenge*. New York: McGraw-Hill, 1982.

Chapter Seven
BRINGING IT OUT INTO THE WORLD—A SHORT COURSE IN MARKETING FOR FREELANCERS

Kenichi Ohmae. *The Mind of the Strategist*. New York: Penguin Books, 1982.

Herb Cohen. *You Can Negotiate Anything*. Secaucus, N.J.: Lyle Stuart, 1980.

Joe Girard with Stanley H. Brown. *How to Sell Anything to Anybody*. New York: Warner Books, 1977.

Frank Bettger. *How I Raised Myself from Failure to Success in Selling*. New York: Cornerstone Library, 1949.

Og Mandino. *University Of Success*. New York: Bantam Books, 1982.

David Ogilvy. *Confessions of an Advertising Man*. New York: Ballantine Books, 1963.

Jeffrey Lant. *The Consultants' Kit*. Cambridge, Mass.: JLA Publications, 1981.

Al Ries and Jack Trout. *Positioning: The Battle for Your Mind*. New York: McGraw-Hill, 1981.

Keep in Touch

Phillip Namanworth and Gene Busnar are co-directors of The Freelance Network. If you would like information about our seminars, consultations, and future publications, please contact us at:

> The Freelance Network
> P.O. Box #412
> Old Chelsea Station
> New York, N.Y. 10011

If you have any correspondence, questions, or stories you'd like to relate, please feel free to contact us through The Freelance Network or in care of our publisher.

Index

G

K

L

M